Mancuso's
Small Business Basics

2nd Edition

Start, Buy or Franchise Your
Way to a Successful Business

Joseph R. Mancuso

Sourcebooks, Inc.
Naperville, IL

Published by: **Sourcebooks, Inc.**
P.O. Box 372, Naperville, Illinois, 60566
(630) 961-3900
FAX: 630-961-2168

Editorial: Todd Stocke
Cover Design: Scott Theisen
Interior Design and Production: Scott Theisen, Sourcebooks, Inc.

This publication is designed to provide accurate and authoritative information in regard to the subject matter covered. It is sold with the understanding that the publisher is not engaged in rendering legal, accounting, or other professional service. If legal advice or other expert assistance is required, the services of a competent professional person should be sought.
From a Declaration of Principles Jointly Adopted by a Committee of the
American Bar Association and a Committee of Publishers and Associations

Mancuso, Joseph.
    Mancuso's small business basics: start, buy or franchise your way to successful business / Joseph R. Mancuso.—2nd ed.
        p.   cm.
    Includes index.
    ISBN 1-57071-212-3
    1. Small business—Planning. 2. New business enterprises—Management. 3. Small business—Purchasing. 4. Franchises (Retail trade)—Management. I. Title.
HD62.7.M366   1998
658.02'2—dc21

                                                                        97-50090
                                                                            CIP

Printed and bound in the United States of America.

Paperback — 10 9 8 7 6 5 4 3 2 1

Contents

Introduction

"If you give a person a fish you feed him for a day. If you teach him to fish, you feed him for a lifetime."

This book was written to appeal to start-up entrepreneurs, practicing small businesspeople, and students. It focuses on the three-step process of starting, financing, and managing a business of your own. I believe it is appropriate to call it *Mancuso's Small Business Basics* because I consider these concepts "the fundamentals."

The starting and financing process is what makes a small business unique. Because of this uniqueness, entrepreneurship can be separated from all other aspects of business management. An entrepreneur starts businesses where none previously existed. In the past, they may have been labeled a hustler, but the American capitalistic system has legitimized them under the umbrella of the French-derived word *entrepreneur.*

All successful business starters have to raise money at some time in the business's growth. Several entrepreneurs, however, claim the money raising process would be better labeled "Russian Roulette." The central part of this book addresses the heart of the financing issue, and for that matter, the heart of the business—the business plan.

What makes this book different is its unique focus on the entrepreneur and the business plan. On the one hand, it can serve as a practical and useful guide to existing enterprises; on the other, it can also serve as a textbook on starting, financing, and the management aspects of running a small business.

Managing an ongoing growth-oriented business, whether your own or someone else's, requires unique management expertise. Just because an individual was a successful manager in a larger business is no guarantee that those management skills are transferable to a small venture.

Even with the U.S. economy in the doldrums for the last five years, it's been commonplace for the first 20 years of someone's career to be paid for and developed by large Fortune 500 companies until mid-career. And then the middle manager gets "downsized." This has created an unparalleled crisis within the U.S. economy.

The Chinese symbol for crisis combines the two symbols for opportunity and danger. What are these "downsized" people to do? They're not in a good position to switch to another large company because they are also probably downsizing. And before they hire from the outside, they tend to promote from within wherever possible. Consequently, downsized executives are opting to operate their own businesses. They have found opportunity within the danger of unemployment.

This book is the first one they should read. The motivation behind these entrepreneurs is their desire to be their own boss. The bureaucratic baloney and the politics have worn down their need to achieve, and they wonder if dedicating their career to a large, unfeeling corporation is really worth the retirement party and the gold watch. These people don't have a strong personal desire to start a business. They don't have a burning cause or issue. Fundamentally, they are seeking independence. This book is written to serve them.

But whether you're at mid-career, or closer to the beginning or end, *Mancuso's Small Business Basics* is designed to get you on your feet in your business venture. With the entrepreneurial market continuing to grow in numbers—and grow more competitive—you can't afford not to hit the ground running.

Motivation

To get into your own business, you have three basic choices: The best of three choices depends on you and your interests, as well as on what deal is currently available. Let's start with number one below—*starting a business.*

1) Starting it yourself
2) Buying or investing in one that someone else started
3) Buying a franchise

The Entrepreneur's Life Cycle

Having a business of your own is not too different from having a child. You experience many of the same emotions and problems. And, as with a child, starting one is half the fun. However, only being a business starter is less than one half of the job. The hard part is to make a business successful.

All successful small businesses start with an idea and proceed through the classic entrepreneur's life cycle. Below is a life cycle for entrepreneurs.

Stage I   The entrepreneur's early development
Stage II   The idea stage
Stage III   The start-up problem

Stage IV	The venture financing
Stage V	The growth crisis
Stage VI	The maturity crisis
Stage VII	The impossible transition

One of the interesting aspects of small businesses is the team built around the entrepreneur. A talented entrepreneur recognizes that the central fact of management is "accomplishing tasks through other people." An ineffective entrepreneur tries to do everything himself. This raises the classic issue of delegating, which is often contrary to the entrepreneur's natural tendencies.

The vast majority of successful small companies were built around an entrepreneurial team and not a single entrepreneur. In fact, partnerships are an increasingly effective method of balancing each entrepreneur's strengths and weaknesses to produce a well-balanced top management team.

Some of the most successful companies were launched by two equal partners who complement one another. Rolls and Royce, the founders of the prestigious British motor car company bearing their names, were totally opposite in philosopies and lifestyles. One was Mr. Inside and the other Mr. Outside, but together they were an effective entrepreneurial team. The same holds for the largest consumer goods company, Procter & Gamble. The team allows balance and strength to exist in the enterprise. The stronger the team, the more powerful the company. It's the synergistic concept of two plus two being equal to five.

Franklin Delano Rooservelt summed up the process this way, "I'm not the smartest fellow in the world, but I can sure pick smart colleagues." He claimed, "Because I'm not so smart, I have to surround myself with real talent." The entreprenuer who can adopt this same philosophy will select the following members of the team:

1) Partners
2) The Godfather
3) Lawyers
4) Advertising Agencies
5) Accountants
6) Bankers
7) Board of Directors

8) Management Consultants
9) Manufacturer's Representatives
10) The Controller

Following is a commentary on the roles of these team members. I shall also try to provide insight into the process of building a team of professionals.

1) Partners

A partner can be a blessing or a curse. Whether you take one or more into your business venture depends on your needs for additional depth in management, marketing, technology, or financing.

Selecting your business partners is not much different from choosing your spouse, and it should be done with the same care. More, perhaps, because the wrong partner can put the entire venture in jeopardy. Marriages are relatively easy to start. A marriage license and a blood test only cost a few dollars. If one fails, you can try again. In business it's not so easy.

I advise finding a partner whose talents complement your own, but whose business philosophy, personality, and background differ. The most successful companies are formed with two partners whose combined abilities give depth to the enterprise, and whose differing backgrounds serve as a buffer against excesses of any kind. You may disagree and you may have conflicts, but usually they are over business issues rather than personalities. A good marketing/financial person is an ideal partner for a strong production/engineering type, but two optimists or two pessimists can kill a business before it has a chance to get off the ground.

Once you have selected your partner, you should immediately agree to disagree. From my experience in mediating between partners, I never become concerned about disagreements. They are akin to fights between alley cats; after all the scrapping, the only result seems to be more cats. The success of a partnership depends on arriving at sensible business decisions through cooperation and equal participation.

2) The Godfather

Every partnership should have a "godfather." Not the kind made famous in Mario Puzo's novel about the underworld, but one who is trusted and respected by both partners and who can serve as a mediator to help resolve conflicts. This helps unstick the sticky problems in the 50-50 partnerships.

This "godfather" should be unbiased; he or she should have little or no vested interest in the company. This person can be a business acquaintance, a friend, a college professor, or someone respected in the technology of your business. Bring him into the picture right at the beginning and keep him abreast of what goes on so he can understand the causes of any problems.

If you are lucky and if the situation is very unusual, you may never require this person to do more than settle minor disputes or serve as a sounding board for new ideas. If worst comes to worst, however, and you must dissolve the partnership, the "godfather" may be the only one who can keep the pieces together long enough for the company to gain its equilibrium and survive. Remember, nothing lasts forever. But the business, if it survives at all, will most likely outlive the partnership.

3) Lawyers

How to Form Your Own Corporation Without a Lawyer for Under $50 (now $75), is a book written by my good friend Ted Nicholas. He has sold more than a million copies of this book and seems to imply that incorporating a small business can be a homemade process. I don't disagree. It can be done cheaper on your own, but I suggest that the first step in starting a business game is to see a lawyer. Not just so he or she can incorporate the business to avoid the legal disadvantages in a proprietorship, but to begin a long relationship. Selecting a proprietorship as the title form of your new business can leave you and your assets exposed to lawsuits by unsatisfied creditors. Using a corporate format will strongly discourage unsecured creditors from suing any individual of the management to collect unsecured, unpaid corporate bills. A corporation will seldom protect an individual from repaying secured bank debt, as almost all banks require a small businessperson to sign two ways: first as the president of the corporation and, second, as an individual. Hence, secured creditors such as banks receive payment from either the corporation or the individual responsible for the management of the business. Unsecured creditors, traditionally known as the accounts payable, are legally discouraged from pursuing any management individual to collect unsecured debts. This level of legal protection for a corporation is not available to a sole proprietor, and often the small businessperson is responsible for all debts, secured and unsecured. It's not the money you save that counts, but the headaches you avoid by having competent legal advice from the beginning. I say step one in the start-a-business process is to see a good lawyer. You can still buy Ted Nicholas's book, but I would not recommend any homemade legal advice.

The lawyer is one of the critical elements in any business. He or she is a full-fledged team member, and many times he captains the team. Hence, he or she must be well qualified. I'd suggest going into the city to select your lawyer and choosing the Securities and Exchange Commission or corporate specialist at one of the prestigious law firms. Your lawyer will know how to take companies public, how to set up tax shield stock plans, and how to keep all the liabilities to a minimum (form and name of the enterprise). One good lawyer is worth a dozen bad ones; a good lawyer is one of the most important and critical players on your management team.

4) Advertising Agencies

Most entrepreneurs tend to avoid advertising agencies, or they put off hiring one until they hit an impasse in their marketing plans. Then it may be too late. I believe in finding a good, small (no more than ten people) agency early.

With advertising agencies, unlike law firms or public accounting firms, the largest is not always the best for the small businessperson. With a small agency, you'll get the attention—and probably plenty of it—of the top person.

The agency is often a junior member of the team, but they should be selected early. An integrated corporate communications concept for letterheads, business cards, envelopes, and logos will establish a corporate identity that blends well together. It makes a big difference when all the corporate communications are well-coordinated from the beginning. It avoids the embarrassment of not looking professional or of not being taken seriously.

Once you've found the right advertising agency, give them their head. Don't tell them what colors you like. Be candid and honest, and give them all the information you can about your product and your markets, but don't impose your artistic talents. The more you give them, the more they'll be able to give you.

When it comes to agency compensation, don't rely on the old fifteen percent of the media costs method. This old method of compensating for agency efforts was very simple. Most approved media will allow an accredited agency to deduct a 15% discount, very much like the airlines allow a travel agency a 15% discount. Hence, an advertising agency that annually placed $100,000 of media billing for a client would be indirectly compensated by paying the various media $85,000 while billing the client the published rates of $100,000. First of all, it's impossible for an agency to work profitably on a straight commission basis unless your media expenditures are considerable. Remember, they are in business to make a profit, too. Furthermore, it tends to create a conflict of interest for the agency, since it is to their advantage if your advertising dollars go into a commissionable media. The best course for your company may be direct mail or some other noncomissionable medium. Do you want the agency working for your company or for the commissionable advertising media? There is a possible conflict between what is good for the media and what is good for the client. An agency that is singularly reimbursed for commission media, print or electronic, may be unreceptive to designing brochures or trade literature because the printing commissions may be less than the earned discount from the commissionable media. An estimate of the annual advertising budget should be the foundation for determining an agency's compensation. This allows a fuller, fairer choice of the optimal allocations between commissionable and noncommissionable activities.

The most practical and fair method of agency compensation is a monthly retainer fee which amounts to about ten percent more than the commissions they would receive on annual forecasted commissionable media expenditures. This method eliminates the conflict of interest and lets the agency worry about what's best for you, not about what's best for them.

5) Accountants

Another person you'll want to get on board at the earliest moment is a top-flight certified public accountant (CPA). Numbers are the language of business management, and intelligent decisions require an understanding of the quantitative factors involved.

If you have hopes for expansion or for going public, line up one of the big accounting firms. A merely adequate accountant is suicide. A big, well-known firm immediately lends credibility to your numbers; and when the time comes for that public offering, three years of audited statements from one of the big names adds plenty of status. Don't worry about a big firm being too expensive. Most of them have separate divisions for small businesses. They'll set up a one-write check system (which can save hours of work and improve your accuracy) and an accounts payable voucher register (so you'll know who you owe money to), proof of your receivables (so you'll know who owes you money), and all the necessary financial systems to help you avoid unnecessary false starts.

Next, introduce your lawyer and your accountant to your banker. There will be plenty of decisions where their functions overlap, so they should know one another from the outset.

6) Bankers

Pick a banker, not a bank. If he or she is with a large bank or a bank with a captive small business investment company (SBIC), so much the better. Many bankers are really venture capitalists in disguise, and they can be sources of valuable financial assistance.

Here again, forget the big titles and pick a young loan officer or assistant vice president, then gain his or her confidence. Supply him or her with detailed pro forma cash flow projections to show what your cash needs will be. Simply stated, this is a cash plan which estimates the future incoming cash and subtracts the estimated future cash needs of the business. The difference will be the estimated future cash needs (or excess cash) generated by the business. Then meet or exceed your projections. Getting financial aid will be easy from then on.

In working with your friendly banker, you'll soon learn that he or she expects you to countersign your company's bank debt personally. Don't let it throw you. It's the only way they have to certify your numbers and your confidence in what you're doing. But don't take this responsibility lightly either. It's easy for you to be overly optimistic, and that can get you into a lot of trouble. Before you sign that note, take a good, hard look at those figures again. That signature on the back of the note isn't an autograph—unless you become very, very famous. The countersignature on a bank note means that you, as an individual, are personally responsible for the debts. In the event that the business goes into bankruptcy and is unable to meet the financial obligation which bears your countersignature, the lender can seek the difference between what is collected and what is owed from you as the countersigner of the debt.

If you have inventory and/or receivables, you may be able to avoid the countersignature, or you may at least be able to limit your personal vulnerability by assigning them to the bank. If the worst happens and the bank has to go after your security, it is better that the bank secures the company's inventory, not your spouse's wedding band. Some states protect your home from creditors or bankers trying to collect against a bankrupt company under the Homestead Act. The Homestead Act originated years ago to protect farmers who often lost their farms when they were unable to meet the payments for large farm equipment. The states individually passed legislation in the 1800s that protected a person's primary residence from creditors other than the principal mortgage holder. But, to gain this level of additional protection, a short two-page document must be filed prior to any seizure attempts by creditors. It's very complicated, very legal, and it varies from state to state; all of these issues point out the reason you selected a good lawyer first. Ask your lawyer how to do it—that's why lawyers are paid so well.

7) Board of Directors

There is no doubt that the most crucial single personification of an entrepreneur's management team is the board of directors. A board of directors is charged with establishing policy level decisions. A well-balanced board of directors adds depth to a small, understaffed enterprise. When the board is composed of respected business advisors who meet periodically and debate policy and develop corporate strategies, then the company is operating on a solid foundation.

Unfortunately, too many small businesses do not have an actual board of directors. The entrepreneur who is concerned with day-to-day activities often ignores the potential advantages of establishing a balanced board of directors. The board of directors is often comprised of a wife and father who never influence business issues. They are rubber stamps in the true sense of the word.

Whether to choose accountants, lawyers, bankers, or others to serve on the board of directors is a puzzle with no single answer. Rather, the answer depends on the other talents of the individuals and on the needs of the company. The only group which consistently offers a universal appeal as board members is a group affectionately labeled "angels." These seasoned investors and businesspeople are often the nucleus of a good working board of directors.

Angels are hard to find, but they do exist. They're those marvelous people who descend from the heavens just to invest in small companies. No, they're not supernatural. Usually they are just successful, wealthy businesspeople, who, instead of putting their money in the stock market, investing in mutual funds, or buying savings bonds, invest a portion of their wealth in young businesses.

This is the best sort of investor/director. Such an individual usually joins the team at the founding level and stays with the company until it makes a public offering. Often, he or she makes useful contacts for the company. When more money is needed, they are usually the first to step forward. Most angels have invested between $100,000 and $200,000 in several small businesses, keeping their stake in each venture below $50,000. They are likely to be the only nonemployee investors in the companies. To top it off, they're usually the salt of the earth—nice people, but smart. As venture capitalists, they are better to do business with than with any other alternative. They don't value their advice as a professional venture capitalist, even though it's usually better. They don't value their money as highly as a professional venture capitalist because they don't have large fixed costs for offices and the like. Compared to doctor and lawyer money, angels are seldom nervous or irrational over business problems because they grew up in business, not in law or medicine. If you can find them (in a city the size of Boston there are probably only 100 angels), you can't go wrong by bringing them into the financing arrangements. Then go the extra step to involve them in a balanced board of directors which meets monthly to debates business policies.

8) Management Consultants

Entrepreneurs, more than other businesspeople, rely on other people such as professional management consultants, college professors, other company presidents, or anyone else who can intelligently offer advice and objectivity.

These people serve as sounding boards for the entrepreneur's ideas and help him or her weigh alternatives before making the final decision. In other fields—such as government, the military, and even sports—these sounding boards exist internally in the form of staff assistants.

Since small businesses can't afford droves of staff assistants, they have to rely on external sources, and this has led to the emergence of professional management consultants for small businesses. The management consultant (M.C.) is usually a person with a broad range of knowledge in the management of businesses, and he or she applies that experience to your problems in order to guide you in the right direction. Ultimately, the decision is always yours; but the M.C. plays a vital role in helping you see flaws and correct them before you implement the plan. The M.C. also is often the source for new creative concepts.

Strangely enough, many small businesses use the services of management consultants successfully. They can often provide the frosting on the cake, but should never be overextended to provide the cake. That's the job of the entrepreneur. This is often confusing or misunderstood by a struggling small businessperson who is unsure of the economic return from a small business consultant. If the business succeeds, it's because of the entrepreneur, not the adviser—the same if it fails. Consultants only provide help, guidance, and assistance; they are never the pivotal difference between success and failure in a small growing enterprise. That's the job of the entrepreneur.

9) Manufacturer's Representatives

The manufacturer's representative, or "rep," is the mainstay of the sales force of most small businesses. They are independent businesspeople, entrepreneurs in their own right, peddling the merchandise of several manufacturers rather than just one.

Reps don't add to a company's fixed costs. They're paid on a commission basis according to what they sell. Because of this, a small company can afford to maintain a respectable sales force without incurring large fixed overhead costs.

Reps are also a valuable source of industry intelligence. They are kind of mercenary soldier, stomping through the industrial mud as a commissioned member of several armies. If anyone knows what's going on, they do. They are the sages of their industries.

When you latch onto a good rep (there are some poor ones), hold onto him or her, even when it's time to hire an inside person. Many companies make special arrangements with their best reps to keep them on. It's good for the company, and it's good for the rep, who lives in fear of selling himself right out of a good line. If a rep performs too well in a territory, many small companies get confused and suddenly believe that the best alternative would be to fire the rep and hire a direct salaried salesperson. A manufacturer may eventually decide that a certain territory is lucrative enough to support a full-time company employee. This cost-efficient decision will occur at different levels for different companies and products. A cost-efficient decision is elusive in practice, but easily explained in theory. It's elusive because the opening assumption usually proves to be misleading. The question is, given the same sales in both cases, when is an independent, commissioned agent less expensive than a salaried full-time company salesperson? The answer is, of course, when less commissions are paid to the agents than salary which would have been paid to the salespeople for a given level of sales. Whenever the crossing point occurs for a sales territory, it is commonly thought to be more cost-efficient to replace the commissioned agent with a salaried employee; but always watch out for the assumptions.

It is useful to clarify this issue in the early stages of business growth, because many small companies begin with manufacturer's representatives and eventually shift to full-time, company-paid salespeople. The issue is: What are the trade-offs in making these decisions? There are both qualitative and quantitative reasons to prefer one type of sales force to another. The qualitative advantages of each are listed below.

Reps

1) A commissioned agent who receives compensation only when he or she sells something.
2) Usually the representative firm has a number of persons covering a single territory instead of just one person.
3) A manufacturer's representative also sells products for other manufacturers, and this can help them in merchandising complementary products.
4) The nature of their specialization makes them knowledgeable about their territory and their customers.
5) The marketing effort by a team of experienced reps is usually more efficient than a headquarters directed effort at identifying and merchandising.

Company Salespeople

1) Their loyalty undoubtedly rests with the single employer and is not scattered among many manufacturers.
2) They are willing to invest effort to develop new products or to maintain service to customers, both of which may be less income productive than pursuing other activities.
3) They can be more efficient above a certain sales volume.
4) You are able to develop better inside managers by leaving them to initially perform at field sales.
5) You are able to control sales activities better.

10) The Controller

Show me a successful small company with great growth potential, and I'll show you a company with a talented financial person keeping his or her thumb on the cash flow—the company controller. This is the person who passes on all company expenditures. They are also the ones who manage to get the quarterly audit done, in spite of last quarter's foolish mistakes.

When given the chance, the controller will vote "no" 80 percent of the time. He frustrates everyone with his pessimism, and he is accused of throwing cold water on every good idea. Production doesn't like him because he refuses to sign purchase orders. Sales doesn't like him because he gives them a hard time about expense reports.

The controller is never popular—he doesn't smile or tell jokes—but he's the one person in the company who can provide the balance it needs. With him, there's temperance. Without him, there could be a drunken spending spree that might cripple a small, young company or a growing old one. This financial genius, along with the first mate, are the two most crucial picks in your draft of management talent.

Entrepreneurs often make fatal mistakes in selecting the financial specialist. This is especially true of technical types. Typically, they are unfamiliar with finance, as compared to their extensive engineering and technical knowledge. Hence, in selecting the financial genius, they often rely on those with college degrees rather than on those with proven experience on the job.

Consequently, technical entrepreneurs hire business school MBAs (Masters in Business Administration) because it's the thing to do, especially if those hired are finance majors. Entrepreneurs tend to be infatuated with the MBA—the brash kid in his late twenties who knows all the answers and all the buzz-words like "game plan" and "M.B.O." (Management by Objectives, a managing technique made famous by Mr. Peter Drucker).

The trouble with most of today's business school graduates is that they have more answers than there are questions. It may sound strange, but too many solutions can create a problem. Furthermore, it's claimed they get too much money and change jobs too often.

In my experience with MBAs in small business, I have found that they spend most of their time analyzing their employer and the company. The ones who excel in small business management are running their own companies. They won't work for entrepreneurs; they *are* entrepreneurs. Think twice before you offer an unusually high salary for a would-be soothsayer.

If you must hire one of the new MBAs, try to find one who is in his or her second or third job. A little experience under the belt could do you a lot of good. A person with an MBA in finance or marketing who is looking for her third job and who has some small company experience could be the right medicine for your company. This is especially true for retail businesses because of the unique nature of retailing. In retailing, it's often best to wait until the MBA is past the age of 40, regardless of the number of previous jobs. A certain maturity plus an MBA is extremely powerful medicine, even for certain sick businesses.

Problem Solving

Entrepreneurial persuaders are always open to outside opinions. They do not act emotionally or out of control. They gather facts, seek advice from trusted advisers, and only then do they make firm decisions. The sequence seems to go like this:

1) Define the problem
2) Develop a list of alternatives
3) Establish the criteria for solutions
4) Seek advice from knowledgeable and involved peers
5) Make a decision and take action
6) Take actions to reinforce the decision and make it work
7) Repeat the cycle again

This process breaks big problems into small problems, which are always easier to handle. Step 5 is what seems to separate the entrepreneurial persuader from others who are also effective problem solvers.

Notice that Step 4 above is the only one that theoretically could be skipped in the model sequence. It adds time and the solution with Step 4 included takes a little longer. But when peer discussion is part of the process, it lowers the probability that you'll have to tackle the same decision multiple times (Step 7).

The Entrepreneur's First Mate

Since entrepreneurial persuaders are effective people with high achievement drives (I like to call them the "ready-fire-aim" types), which personality type works best with them? Let's examine a four-quadrant matrix composed of the following choices:

Look at number one, lazy and stupid. No need to spend a lot of time on this choice, as anyone who is lazy and stupid shouldn't even be in private enterprise. They flourish in government.*

The second choice would be someone stupid and energetic, but this isn't a good match either. While we are empathetic to the stupid part, it's the energetic component that drives normal folks nuts. Incidentally, people who are energetic and stupid do not just work in government, they are government leaders.

Most people think that the third choice, someone who is bright and energetic, would be the ideal first mate for an entrepreneurial persuader. They couldn't be more incorrect. After all, entrepreneurial persuaders are also bright and energetic, and choosing a first mate who is just the same is like adding gasoline to a blazing fire. What the fire needs is a wet cloth to keep it in control and to act as a damper. Two bright energetics will spoil any activity. It's like having two captains of a ship, two orchestra conductors, or two quarterbacks trying to run a football team. It can't be done. They have the same goals, but they always have different methods.

Of the three types discussed so far, bright energetics are actually the worst choice of all because they can cost you everything. In contrast, people who are stupid and lazy cost you only what you are paying them. Those who are stupid and energetic can cost you what you are paying them plus damages. Compared to someone who is bright and energetic, which could cost you the whole thing, they are both cheap alternatives.

Choose number four; people who are bright and lazy are easily the most valuable commodity in the American enterprise system. We don't have enough of them. There happens to be an excess of entrepreneurial persuaders, but they are optimized only when they work in combination with a bright and lazy person. The shortage in the U.S economy is not among the bright and energetics, but rather the bright and lazies.

A bright and lazy person understands very quickly what has to be done. Full instructions are never necessary. However, the most valuable trait in this personality is really the lazy aspect. Lazy in this context doesn't mean no good; it means slow down.

*The Lord's Prayer is composed of 50 words. The Gettysburg Address is composed of 266 words. The Ten Commandments have 297 words. And a recent government proclamation setting the price of cabbage had 26,911 words.

Here is an example of the value of a bright and lazy vice president working for an entrepreneurial persuader who is growing a business.

Entrepreneurial persuaders like to arrive at work several hours early because that's the best time to sell. They have discovered that between 6 and 9 a.m. they can get a lot of work done with no phones ringing and no one there to bother them. By nine o'clock, they have enough work compiled to keep ten people busy for a year.

A "bright and lazy" arrives at the office at around 10:30. The entrepreneurial persuader meets him or her at the door and follows the person all the way over to his or her desk, barking hundreds of instructions, commands, jobs, and missions. They eagerly transfer piles of papers to this first mate and then head back to their office to create another massive pile of work.

What does the bright and lazy vice president do with the first set of papers and instructions? Usually, he or she lets them sit. By noon, the entrepreneurial persuader comes rushing back into the first mate's office with another massive pile of work. In excited tones, the persuader sweeps the first pile off the desk and places down the second. He says in a panting voice to the bright and lazy vice president (who is busy calling home, reading *The Wall Street Journal*, or having a cup of coffee), "You know what I told you this morning? Forget all that." In combination with a bright and lazy first mate, a rainmaker doesn't make any acid rain.

Motivational Profile

While the following traits characterize people who start businesses, I have been searching for three decades for one trait that was a single foolproof indicator. It had to be an accurate but quick litmus test.

In 1986, at my 25-year Worcester Polytechnic Institute (WPI) college reunion, I hit upon it. It has not yet stood the test of time, but it looks good so far. Here's how to tell:

- Entrepreneur—Gets in the car and drives off. While driving, he or she adjusts the radio, air conditioner, lights, seats, mirror, and seat belt. All of this is done at some peril as the car reaches maximum speed.

- Hired hand—Adjusts the radio, air conditioner, lights, seats, mirror and seat belt, then starts the car and drives off.
- Passenger—To make the test infallible, the entrepreneur needs to be a passenger in a car operated by a hired hand. Some of them can't do it because it involves giving up too much control, but here's what happens when they are passengers.

As the driver adjusts the radio, mirror, air conditioning, seat, seat belt, and vents, the entrepreneur-passenger uncontrollably shouts out, *"For God's sake, start the car!"*

So far, it looks like my Rosetta stone.

The Synergy of the Entrepreneur

After fighting a five-day battle, an American soldier walked nearly 75 miles through the French countryside to a small village of about 50 homes. He was so tired and hungry, he could hardly raise his hand to knock on the door. An angry woman opened the door and demanded to know the nature of his business. He asked for a piece of bread, a glass of water, or anything she could spare. She screamed at him to go away, saying she could hardly feed herself as she angrily slammed the door in his face.

The soldier then walked to a second house and asked for food or water. The owner refused even more angrily than the woman in the first house.

So the soldier walked a bit farther until his gaze fell on a cracked, but nevertheless functioning, water fountain in the middle of the town square.

The soldier drank as much water as his stomach could hold and, in the middle of the park, started a small fire. He filled his helmet with water, placed two average-sized stones in it and began stirring the mixture over the fire.

A little boy approached and asked what he was doing. The soldier replied, "I am making the most delicious stone soup in the whole world." The boy asked if he could have some. "Certainly," the soldier replied, "but the soup needs a few vegetables to make it really delicious." The boy said his parents had a few carrots at home and ran to get them. Meanwhile, a married couple came along and asked the soldier what he was doing. "I am making the most delicious stone soup in the whole world." They asked if he would share his bounty with them, and he replied, "Of course, but I need a soup bone and perhaps some spices to make this soup the very best." The wife rushed home to find something to contribute to the mixture. While she was gone, an old woman passed through and helped the mixture by adding a few potatoes. Within an hour, several more people had contributed to the soup.

At just the right moment, the starving soldier removed the stones and ladled out a cup of marvelous stone soup to each person who had contributed ingredients. There still was plenty left over for him to enjoy.

In this children's story, the soldier is a catalyst who brings these individuals together for their mutual gain. None of those who enjoyed the delicious soup had the ingredients to make it individually. The soldier's ingenuity brought everyone together for the common good. This illustrates synergy and entrepreneurship at its best.

Chapter 2

Preparing the Business Plan

What Is a Business Plan?

A document written to raise money for a growing company is known as a business plan. The most popular types are written for entrepreneurial companies seeking a private placement of funds from venture capital sources. Internal venture management teams of larger companies also write business plans. Although these venture plans seldom circulate to external private placement sources, they do progress upward within the organization for approval by corporate management.

Modest differences exist between entrepreneurial and internal venture group plans. The major differences rest in the risk and reward structure and not in the reading or writing of the document. The objectives of both types of plans are the same—launching a new business or expanding a promising small business. The ultimate responsibility for success or failure in one case rests with an entrepreneur/venture capitalist and in the other with a manager/vice president. But no matter what its origin, the document that consummates the financing is called the business plan. In both cases, the document must be thorough and well done to be successful in securing new capital.

The vast majority of business plans, however, are prepared by entrepreneurs seeking venture capital. New venture groups within large companies are expanding their activities, but they do not approach the number of existing small companies seeking the same goal. As a comparison, there are about 14 million small businesses in the U.S., while only several thousand larger companies exist in this country. In addition, start-up companies, which still appear despite current depressed economic conditions, require a special breed of entrepreneurial business plan. This third category of brand-new companies is the least common source of business plans.

The term "business plan" is the more formal name for the document. However, many within the financial and legal communities prefer the nickname "deal." Although the latter is crude and a bit harsh, it does have shock value, which makes it a realistic and descriptive phrase. Some financiers carry this nicknaming one step further and compare the fundraising process to the television program "Let's Make A Deal." In any case, the word "deal," which embodies the excitement of the chase, becomes "business plan" when the chase is successfully completed.

The Plan

Why should you go to the trouble of creating a written business plan? There are three major reasons:

1) The process of putting a business plan together, including the thought put in before beginning to write it, forces you to take an objective, critical, and unemotional look at your business project in its entirety.
2) The finished product—your business plan—is an operating tool which, properly used, will help you manage your business and work toward its success.
3) The completed business plan is the means for communicating your ideas to others and provides the basis for your financing proposal.

The importance of planning cannot be overemphasized. By taking an objective look at your business, you can identify areas of weakness and strength, pinpoint needs you might otherwise overlook, spot problems before they arise, and begin planning how you can best achieve your business goals. As an operating tool, your business plan helps you establish reasonable objectives and figure out how to best accomplish them. It also helps you red-flag problems as they arise and aids you in identifying their source, thus suggesting ways to solve them. It may even help you avoid some problems altogether.

In order for it to work, it is important that *you* do as much of the work as possible. A professionally prepared business plan won't do you any good if you don't understand it thoroughly. This understanding comes from being involved with its development from the very start.

No business plan, no matter how carefully constructed and no matter how thoroughly understood, will be of any use at all unless you use it. Going into business is rough—over half of all new businesses fail within the first two years of operation; over 90% fail within the first ten years. A major reason for failure is lack of planning. The best way to enhance your chances of success is to plan and to follow through on your planning.

Use your plan. Don't put it in the bottom drawer of your desk and forget all about it.

Your business plan can help you avoid going into a business venture that is doomed to failure. If your proposed venture is marginal at best, the business plan will show you why and may help you avoid paying the high tuition of business failure. It is far cheaper not to begin an ill-fated business than to learn by experience what your business plan could have taught you at a cost of several hours of concentrated work.

Finally, your business plan provides the information needed by others to evaluate your venture, especially if you will need to seek outside financing. A thorough business plan automatically becomes a complete financing proposal that will meet the requirements of most lenders.

Preparing a Business Plan for Lenders or Investors

This is a true story. In the late 1960s, a sightless entrepreneur raised $2 million at a luncheon with the partners of one of New York's most prestigious investment banking firms. The purpose was to launch a new company whose objective was to merge computer technology and education to solve social problems. I don't mean the partners of the investment banking firm set off after lunch to raise $2 million. I mean that following the dessert, the entrepreneur left the luncheon with a certified check for $2 million in his hands. Nothing like this in the annals of venture capital has happened before or since, so don't hold your breath until it happens again!

The late 1960s were fascinating times on Wall Street. Venture capital could be raised for any purpose via a public offering. The stock price of any new company from 1967 to mid-1969 went up. One prospectus from that era described the background of a man and his wife, each about 23 years of age, who intended to use the proceeds of the public offering to identify and promote a new business. The prospectus, or business plan, provided no more information than that. The public poured millions of dollars into small underwriting to launch companies whose names they did not know. Little or no due diligence was performed by the brokerage firms that were underwriting these new issues. Today, most of the new companies of the late 1960s and their underwriters are out of business, and the public is reluctant to return to a stock market that costs so dearly. The process of launching a new company is considerably different.

As the 1960s passed into the early 1970s, private venture capital firms became the primary source of start-up and expansion capital. The new issue public market was laid to rest. For example, in 1974, the only new issue I can remember was that of a small firm whose business was liquidating brokerage firms. Between 1975 and 1976 there were a handful of new issues, and in 1977 and 1978, perhaps twenty. The few private venture capitalists, beaten about their wallets by the stock market's decline, began to demand substantially more information from entrepreneurs about their objectives, the costs of achieving those objectives, and a myriad of other details. In addition, someone had to take the blame for the huge portfolio losses. Rather than blaming themselves for their Koros, Ubris, and Ate, as would the good Spartans carrying their dead on their shields, the venture capitalists of the early 1970s pinned the blame on the entrepreneurs. They told them, in effect, "I'll finance your company, but I have to own most of the stock, and I must have voting control of the board." This did not encourage new company formation, although a few interesting enterprises were launched between 1973-1975. The primary effect of this attitude was to reduce the number of new companies launched in the early 1970s, shrink the number of venture capitalists, and usher in competitive government programs to assist in new company formation.

The 1990s

The venture capital industry is new, immature, and seemingly in perpetual transition. This industry is constantly trying to grasp and absorb the various changes that affect it. Entrepreneurs are not aware of this. All too frequently, entrepreneurs think that a venture capitalist is J.P. Morgan or Jacob Schiff reincarnate: very wealthy, ultra-conservative, and poised to press a buzzer under the desk that will call in a runner with bags of cash to pour on the table for the entrepreneur to scoop up. Not true! Venture capitalists are intelligent young men and women seeking to simultaneously recommend to their investment committees the next Syntex, Polaroid, or Xerox and prevent erosion of capital in their fund through portfolio demise. Therefore, when an entrepreneur and a venture capitalist meet, the entrepreneur should bear in mind the following idea:

a) The venture capitalist wishes that the information he or she is given by the entrepreneur is true.

b) The venture capitalist, if sold, must resell the idea to his or her investment committee and must be given the facts with which to do so.

c) The venture capitalist has 20 other situations on his or her desk, each competing for time and attention.

d) Venture capitalists make judgments about a new company's projections based on their recollection of past projections, both realized and unrealized.

The latter is a process similar to the description in Plato's *Republic* of the artisans in the cave chained in place all day staring at shadows. They are not permitted to turn around and see the shadow-caster—they can only stare straight ahead at the shadow—but they must form judgments about the shadowcasters based on the shadows.

Similarly, venture capitalists literally stare at projections all day, unable to see the actual future operating statement numbers. If the projections remind the venture capitalists of the sales and earnings trends of Intel, City Investing, or Teledyne, he or she will be inclined to dig into the deal. If they evoke memories of Stirling Homex or Viatron, the venture capitalist will not be so inclined.

The uncertainty surrounding the entrepreneur is the ability to realize the projections. He or she may be merely a good projections maker and a lousy accomplisher. The venture capitalist does not know which. Herein lies a dichotomy: The venture capitalist tries to attack the business assumptions on which the projections are based to determine their credibility, that is, the ability of the entrepreneur to make the projections come true. The entrepreneur jabs with upside potential. The venture capitalist counters with downside risk. The projections are dissected to their most minute ratio to try to see if the business plan has credibility. The battle lasts on into the night, for day after day, until finally the seller and buyer become joined in their enthusiasm for a new business and have but to agree on a price in order to complete the funding.

This all sounds a bit romanticized, yet there is no denying that raising money is the battle of the war called wealth. It is but an easy battle in a three-to-five-year war, and the entrepreneur has far less experience in fighting it than the venture capitalist. Knowing how to prepare a credible business plan helps put the two on equal footing.

The Five Minute Reader

Business plans are comprehensive documents that often require several months to compile. Although they vary in length and complexity, the process of writing them requires the coordination of external legal, financial, and accounting assistance. In addition, the internal analysis of manufacturing, finance, and marketing must coincide with the external activities. This coordination adds to the time required for preparation. Spending $2,000 to $20,000 for outside services to prepare a business plan is typical. The preparer intuitively believes that the plan's thoroughness and sophistication reflect the enterprise's likelihood for success. Consequently, the tendency is to do the plan well and sometimes do it and redo it.

Despite all this care during the preparation, most business plans are not read in detail from cover to cover. Although five weeks may have been required to compile it, potential investors will initially invest only five minutes reading it. A venture capitalist who receives a dozen plans a day—hundreds annually—simply does not have enough time to read through each one. In fact, a leading venture capitalist at a large Boston bank claims he never reads any plan. "They all say the same thing and it's never true," he comments, "so I never read them."

Multiple exposures are often given to a single business plan, one of the reasons hundreds of deals arrive at a single venture capitalist's office. An entrepreneur in dire need of funds will often mail the plan to a long list of venture capitalists. Such lists are available from several sources. This multiple exposure, frequently described as "shopping the deal," often seriously weakens rather than improves the chances of raising the needed capital. On the other hand, not showing the plan to anyone assures failure.

Incidentally, the Securities and Exchange Commission (SEC) frowns on exposing a deal to more than 35 potential investors. This issue is in constant flux; first you must comply with federal government regulations for an offering, and second, you must comply with each state's so-called blue-sky offering laws. Just as you'd guess, these two regulatory bodies (state and federal government) don't always have common laws. For instance, in Massachusetts, a deal can only be shown to 25 potential investors, while the federal limit is 100 potential investors. Hence, both rules must be observed. Also, these rules vary depending upon the amount of money you seek. Check with your lawyer on this issue because the guidelines are constantly changing.

The number of deals reviewed by a venture capitalist depends on his or her reputation, which in turn depends on past success. Currently, about one thousand venture capital firms exist in the United States, and a little better than one-half are also SBICs, small business investment companies regulated by the federal Small Business Administration (SBA). The number of successes contained within a single venture capital portfolio seldom exceeds one in ten.

A typical million-dollar venture portfolio might be invested in ten companies. Although only one winner is the average, the typical portfolio would have five businesses that are essentially bankrupt; two or three marginal firms with little real potential; and one or two firms with a chance to become big winners. The pattern reveals the danger of the venture business and demonstrates the crucial nature of a single winner.

A venture capitalist heading up the largest bank-owned small business investment company (SBIC) in Boston believes the batting average which is so often quoted by academicians, "mixes up the singles, doubles, and homeruns." A better average would be the slugging percentage, or, in baseball terms, an average that weighs the home runs and triples more than the singles and doubles." In either case, he argues that the ultimate criterion is always based on a return on investment (ROI) analysis. For instance, the typical venture source previously mentioned, with 10 investments of $100,000 each, will have committed $1 million to its portfolio. If all the investments eventually turn sour save one, the batting average will be .100. However, if the one success produces a $2 million gain on its original $100,000 investment, or 20 times return, the slugging average would be calculated as 2:1 or $2 million returned on the total $1 million invested. This, according to the venture capitalists in Boston, accounts for the confusion in analyzing the industry. One success could actually count much higher than a grand slam home run.

Writing for a Five Minute Reader

The primary problem in writing a business plan is making it comprehensive and shaping it for the reader for whom it is intended—the prospective investor with five minutes to read it. The entrepreneur should accept the inevitable: A potential investor will initially invest only five minutes to read a plan. Therefore, the plan should be adapted to this time span.

A central message of how-to-write-a-plan advice is that you should tailor the document to meet the needs and desires of the potential investors. This sound advice does not mean that you should exaggerate, lie, or inflate the sales projections. It does mean that you should emphasize items of special interest for a specific potential investor. A single plan rarely suffices for all possible uses. However, every plan eventually has its moment and is given a once over lightly.

Insight into what happens to a plan when it finally reaches the top of the pile is scarce. What happens during the five minutes the venture capitalist examines the plan? How is it read? How is it analyzed? An understanding of the reading and interpretation process may help to direct the writing style and the focus of the plan. On the basis of field research involving several dozen venture capitalists and several other entrepreneurs, I have concluded that all knowledgeable investors use the precious five minutes of reading time in about the same way.

Preparing the Business Plan

People are always telling me they would like to see the perfect business plan. "Would you mind handing me that business plan over there? Right—the perfect one. You see, I'm in a hurry, and I don't want to spend a whole lot of time writing one, so I'll just take advantage of someone else's hard work. Just show me the perfect plan and I'll copy it."

Can you imagine the results? What you'd end up with would be a program for a word processor that types out, "John went to _____ _____ high school in _____, and then he went to _____ college," and so on. All you do is feed in a few magic words and change the business from computers to a restaurant, or a restaurant to construction, or construction to software, and you're ready to go. The program has all the boilerplate stuff already, so abracadabra, you've got the perfect business plan. In fact, there's a company in Los Angeles that does just that. I'll bet it does pretty good business with accountants, lawyers, and other business plan preparers. As far I'm concerned, a plan like that is just a waste of time. It's like saying, "Let me see a work of art that's perfect. I want to have the Mona Lisa in my house, so give me a paint-by-numbers kit." I remain shocked by the amount of software sold to prepare a business plan.

It's foolish to think that you could paint the Mona Lisa by the numbers. And when it comes right down to it, a business plan is a work of art in its own right. It's the document that personifies and expresses your company. So when people ask me whether it should be five pages or fifty, I answer them by saying, "Who knows?" Some people might type up three-page plans and raise a million dollars. I could show you one that's only seven pages long that raised more than a million. But most business plans are "wheelbarrow" plans. You have to put it in a wheelbarrow to carry it, and that doesn't even include the appendix that you left back at the office.

I like to use the example of someone who was my hero when I was a kid growing up. His name was Joe DiMaggio, and he played baseball for the New York Yankees. The guy looked great and acted great, and when he hit the ball, his swing was level perfect. Even in the outfield, he was a beautiful and graceful person, and his lifetime batting average was .325. At the same time, there was a guy over in St. Louis who stood at the plate with his fanny sticking out, his arms tilted, and his knees bent. It looked like he'd either fall over from the wind off the ball, or get hit by the first ball thrown his way. His name was Stan Musial, and even though his stance was completely different, he had a lifetime batting average of .331. The message is the same when it comes to business plans.

I can't give you a magic formula: "Copy this and you'll have the perfect plan." In fact, the perfect plan is probably one that was turned down. The ones that get financed are seldom perfect, but they are sweet. That's why my advice is called the "Frosting on the Cake Principle." I start out with the assumption that most entrepreneurs can write a business plan that's about an 8 on a scale of 1 to 10—and that's not bad because most business plans aren't even 8s. Most plans are about 6s, but it doesn't really matter whether a plan is an 8, a 4, a 6, or a 2, because the ones that get financed are 10s.

Let's say business plans that are "found in nature" are 8s. As I said, a plan that's an 8 is a good plan, but 8s don't get financed. So if you start with an 8, how do you put the frosting on the cake? Read another book? Go back to fundamentals? That's fine for bringing a 1 up to an 8, but how do you go from an 8 to an 11? It's like golf. It's a lot easier to bring your score to 80 from 100 than it is to bring it down to 70 from 80. It looks like a linear scale, but it's not. An 8 is an entrepreneur's plan that is "found in nature." If you add an accountant and a lawyer, another two months and another three grand, you come up with a 9; but a 9 is no better than a 6 because neither one of them gets financed. So if a 10 is a plan that gets financed, what's an 11? The answer is, an 11 is a plan that's so good you have to turn back money.

If you actually take in too many checks and have to explain to an investor why he or she is being cut out of the deal, that's an 11; and this chapter is designed to tell you how to take a 9 and turn it into an 11 with magic. If you ever did magic tricks as a kid, you'll know what I'm talking about. The first question a magician hears after having done a trick is, "How did you do it?" Eventually if the magician finally gives up and shows how to do it, what does the audience say? "Oh, is that all? I knew that all the time!" So what I'm going to tell you about business plans isn't very different from common sense, but the problem with common sense is that it isn't always that common until someone else explains it.

Nine Questions That Must Be Answered

Before I go any further, it's time for you to do some of the work. Please answer the following questions:

1) What is the single most important aspect of the business plan, according to the venture capitalist?

   _____

2) List, in chronological order, the six steps in presenting a business plan:

   a) _____
   b) _____
   c) _____
   d) _____
   e) _____
   f) _____

3) Name two elements of a business plan which can bring it from the 7 to 9 range up to a 10:

   a) _____
   b) _____

4) List the five questions a venture source needs answered:

   a) _____
   b) _____
   c) _____

d) _____
e) _____

5) In what order are the parts of a business plan read?
a) _____
b) _____
c) _____
d) _____
e) _____
f) _____

6) Rank, in order of importance, the ten sources of linkage people for introducing your deal to venture capital sources:
a) _____
b) _____
c) _____
d) _____
e) _____
f) _____
g) _____
h) _____
i) _____
j) _____

7) Identify the nine members of an entrepreneurial team and highlight the most important player:
a) _____
b) _____
c) _____
d) _____
e) _____
f) _____
g) _____
h) _____
i) _____

8) What should be found on the summary page of the business plan?

a) _____

b) _____

c) _____

d) _____

e) _____

9) What are the six most common debt/equity instruments available to a lender or investor?

a) _____

b) _____

c) _____

d) _____

e) _____

f) _____

Dr. Edward B. Roberts, the David Sarnoff professor of Management and Technology at MIT, did a study of 20 business plans submitted by high-tech, start-up companies to venture capitalists in the Boston area. Here are some of the results of that study:

1) While all 20 plans stated an overall objective, only 14 had a specific strategy that appeared rational and achievable.

2) The central thrust of the plans broke down as follows:

Product	47%
Market	29%
People	24%

3) Profitability and growth were not discussed in detail in 45% of the plans.

4) Three-quarters of the plans failed to identify details about their competitors.

5) The marketing plan was consistently the weakest element of the 20 plans, while the R&D aspect was consistently the strongest.

6) Marketing research and selling were given very low priority in three-quarters of the plans, and little background in these areas was evidenced. (It is interesting to note that earlier research by Professor Roberts showed an inverse relationship between product success and a

firm's ability to do market research. It concludes by stating that if time exists for market research, you're already to late for the market.)

7) The financial projections offered in these plans broke down as follows:

None	10%
Data not available	5%
1-3 year income statement only	10%
4-5 year income statement only	40%
1-3 year income statement and balance sheet	15%
4-5 year income statement and balance sheet	10%

Roberts concludes the report on his research with the following statement: "One critical aspect of the business plan is that if you don't do it right, there is a high likelihood that you will never do anything beyond it. Business planning needs to be undertaken seriously, if for no other reason than it is a major tangible representation of who you are, what you are, and what you want to be to the financial community. It may also even relate to later business success."

Two Tips on Preparing Financials

I'm going to give you two tips on business plan preparation. These are great tips. They won't turn an 8 into an 8.1, and they won't help you to get financed, but you will need them just the same.

For some reason, convention dictates that all the words and romance in a business plan go up front, while the financials are always in the back. I've always thought the front page of a business plan should be the balance sheet, and the back pages should tell where you went to school, what you plan to do, and so on. Instead, the balance sheets always go in the back, so that you have to shuffle the plan around to get to them. All the same, it's those back pages that get read, so the way they are presented is a key issue.

Of course, most entrepreneurs present financial information the same way they present plans—home-cooked. They dream up their financial format in such a way that the balance sheet becomes the hardest part of the plan to read. But bankers and financial people are going to be the people who read your plan, so it pays to prepare it in terms they will understand. When Thomas Edison invented the light bulb, he described it in terms of candle power. By using the already accepted terms to describe his new invention, he made it easier for his invention to gain acceptance. It made the conversion from gas to electricity smoother.

My point is: Prepare your financials in such a way that bankers and financial people will be able to understand them easily. How do you do it? Here is a roundabout explanation. When little commercial bankers want to grow up to be big bankers, they get their training from Robert Morris Associates (sometimes from the American Banking Association), an association of commercial loan officers.* And what do venture capitalists most often share (besides their need to make a profit)? A common background. While entrepreneurs come in all shapes and sizes, venture capitalists all look as if they came out of the same mold.

I always say (and I joke when I say it) that venture capitalists are born with a step-by-step chart to follow. First, they go to prep school, then they go to Princeton, and from there they go on to Harvard Business School. After that, they spend two years at a bank, two or three years with a major consulting firm, then they go to work for an SBIC. After all those steps, by the time they turn 35, they are ready to be stamped "venture capitalist" and go to work with one of the private (non-SBIC) venture funds. While the pattern may not be exactly the same for every venture capitalist, the one thing that they most often have in common is the "two years at the bank." What does that mean? They all have been trained by Robert Morris Associates at one time or another. Robert Morris is the training arm of the banking industry. So when little bankers are trained to become commercial lenders, they are trained on Robert Morris (or Bank Administration Institute) forms.

Therefore, it's helpful to financial people if entrepreneurs prepare their financials on Robert Morris (or equivalent) forms.** These forms contain all three of the fundamental financial tools. The income statement is at the top, the balance sheet is at the bottom, and the glue that holds them together is right in the middle—that's the cash flow statement. On one page you have all three financial forms, so you can get all of the financial information at a glance. It's a one-sweep system,

*Robert Morris Associates, 1616 Philadelphia National Bank Building, Philadelphia, PA 19107
**You may order forms and samples from Bankers Systems, Inc., Box 1457, St. Cloud, MN 56302

and it reminds me of a three-sweep oscilloscope. If you've ever seen a three-sweep oscilloscope, you know if one sweep goes up, one goes down, and one goes sideways; when you sweep them together, you see the interaction. The same goes for financials. Reading them one at a time doesn't give nearly as clear a picture as is gained by watching their interaction.

If you want to have some fun with your banker, put a Robert Morris form in front of him, then count the seconds it takes for his eyes to come to rest on lines 35 and 36. You won't get past 2 because these lines are called cash. That's my message about using a standardized accounting format. The second advantage is best appreciated when the entrepreneur makes a financial presentation to the venture capitalist. This is the same for any of these standardized accounting forms, not just Robert Morris. Your job is to discover the preference of the reader before you prepare your financials.

Now that I've told you all about the Robert Morris forms, let me add one caution. With the arrival of the desktop computer have come the Lotus 1-2-3 fanatics, and the Lotus 1-2-3 fanatics are even worse than their Robert Morris counterparts. While the group is still small, you might try to find out which presentation is preferred. Seven out of ten will want the Robert Morris forms, but those three exceptions won't be comfortable until they see the Lotus 1-2-3 (or equivalent) printout. Also, other programs are now becoming popular, and the Lotus 1-2-3 people may soon outnumber the Robert Morris old-timers.

Tip two is just as valuable as tip one, but it alone won't get your plan financed either. It's called "How You Price the Deal." Remember, if you have the wrong price for the wrong thing, you're in real trouble.

How much stock you give up to obtain how much money is the unanswerable question in a venture capital deal. You don't want to give up too much (after all, it's your money) or too little (after all, it's their money). The final ratio will undoubtedly be determined after some long-term and dead serious negotiating, so it's important that you know this rule of thumb.

1) With most entrepreneurial companies, you simply cannot use price/earnings ratio (P/E) of similar companies

because they will seldom offer an accurate equivalent to your situation.

2) A venture source wants to earn about 45% compounded annual return on all funds invested. Offer them much below 40%, and they're usually not interested. If your projections are much over 60%, they'll become very skeptical. So, in order to get financed, business plans should offer 45% compounded return on investment (ROI). Here's a sample of how that works on a $1 million investment (all figures are millions):

End of Year	Value of Amount Invested
1	1.45 M
2	2.10 M
3	3.05 M
4	4.42 M
5	6.40 M (5th year gain)

3) A 44% compounded ROI is approximately equivalent to six times your money in five years. That's the goal.

4) The total value of your company is determined by multiplying your after-tax earnings in the fifth year by an acceptable (usually low) P/E ratio. The most commonly used P/E ratio is 10.

Hence, if your business projects after-tax earnings of $20 million in the fifth year, and you need $1 million now to launch your venture, how much of the company do you have to surrender to the venture capitalists? The answer is roughly 30%. Now, let's go over the way we arrive at that figure. First, multiply the standard P/E (10) by the after-tax earnings ($2 million). Then figure that if the venture capitalist gives you $1 million in year one, he'll require roughly $6 million in value by the end of the year five. So if the value of the company, given a P/E of 10, is $20 million, and assuming the venture capitalist wants an ROI of about 44%, you will have to give up 30% ($6 million in value) of the company for $1 million in start-up money. That's the arithmetic.

What exactly is a P/E ratio? First it's the price per share divided by the earnings per share. But when an investor looks at a company's P/E, what does he or she see? Sex appeal—the P/E is a company's sex appeal. To an investor, the Ford Motor Company is a little unsexy these days because its P/E is down around 4. IBM, on the other hand, is very sexy because its P/E is up around 18 or 20. Are you beginning to get the picture? Let's talk about one of the sexiest companies of all time: H. Ross Perot's Electronic Data Systems (EDS). When EDS went public, its P/E was 120, that means that for every dollar EDS earned, the value of the company increased by $120! To put that in perspective, let me give you this example. Let's say the Ford Motor Company earned $1 billion last year. On the other hand, EDS earned just 10% of that $100 million, their value would be calculated at $12 billion or three times that of the Ford Motor Company! Now that's what I call a financially sexy company!

Romance and the Business Plan

It is well established that you can't raise money without a business plan. If you ever try to raise money without one, the financial source will listen to your song and dance, then say, "Come back and see us again when your plan is ready." Over the last 10,000 years, God has been working overtime to create people, and in that time he's created all kinds of people. Someone said he created 20 billion people of all sorts, and he created four people a second in 1995. But what has always fascinated me is that in all that time and with all that hard work, God has never created an overfinanced company!

Therefore, every company that has ever existed has had to start with some kind of plan. Maybe it's called a feasibility study or maybe it's called the deal, but it is a business plan by any name. One of the best ways to prepare yourself to prepare a business plan is to remove yourself from your own business. Step back as far as you can and take as objective a look as possible. One good way to help yourself gain this kind of objectivity is to examine other people's business plans before you go to work on your own. However, you should look critically, examine exactly what is there, and try to figure out what is missing. Later you should examine your own plan in the same way.

Here is how money people read a business plan. The thing they're really looking for is the romance, and it's an entrepreneur's job to bring the romance into the plan because most bankers and venture capitalists become bored with looking at the same thing again and again. The financial side will get their attention, but the romance is what is going to do the selling.

Moreover, don't copy someone else's plan, even those you judge to be perfect. Each plan, like every snowflake, must be different. Each is a separate piece of art, each must be reflective of the individuality of the entrepreneur. Just as you wouldn't copy someone else's romancing techniques, you should seek to distinguish your plan for its differences.

However, before I tell you what the romance is, it will help if I tell you one thing that it isn't. It isn't a plan's physical appearance. Entrepreneurs sometimes think they can disguise the flaws in a plan by putting it in a fancy package. I've seen plans that were bound in leather with gold printing on the front and plans with a lot of fancy typesetting, but believe me, if a plan isn't any good, nothing is going to help sell it. In fact, whenever I see a fancy package, it automatically sends up a red flag. I want to know what's wrong with the plan. The plans that are bound as a book are also a red flag.

The romance isn't in what the plan looks like, rather it's in what it says. The romance is the hook, and anyone who knows anything about romance knows what it's like to get hooked. It's the sizzle in the steak, so let's look at what is going to make a venture capitalist fall in love with your plan.

1) A history of success. More than anything else, the venture capitalist wants assurance of success, and nothing succeeds like success. If you (or team members) have done it once, they'll believe you can do it again.

2) A well-recognized market. Cures for cancer or herpes come with an automatic market, a restaurant doesn't. Sure, you say, "But everybody has to eat." Of course, but unless you can show why people will want to eat your food (and I'm talking about an in-depth analysis, not just a few dozen great recipes), you're going to come up short in the romance department.

3) Somebody big is in it. There's no better way to make a venture capitalist fall in love with your plan than to show him that someone else already has. That's not just romance, that's sex appeal. It's the attraction for what others possess.

4) Potential for going public. In this respect, raising capital is a lot like the fashion business. In the fashion business, buyers try to decide what the public is going to want to wear in two years. The venture capitalist wants to speculate that your stock will appeal to public investors in three to seven years. You see, investors need to be liquid and highly profitable too.

5) "I don't want your money as much as I want your advice." This one's tricky, but it has won many an investor. It sounds like flattery, and in a sense it is. The point is that you have to let them know that you want them on your board—that their experience and expertise is at least as necessary to your success as their money is. Don't worry—money always follows advice.

6) If your company dies tomorrow, is the world going to suffer? Before there was a personal computer, no one knew they needed one. Now it's a billion dollar market. If you have a plan for a product that will create a permanent market, you've got the romance.

The People Who Manage Money

The funny thing about money is that the only thing you can't buy with it is money; but you can buy money with stock. The only question is how to come up with the conversion rate to turn your stock into money. H. Ross Perot gives you one share of stock, and you give him $120 (when EDS's P/E ratio was 120), and what you're buying with that $120 is one dollar's worth of earnings. Remember, a good story is worth more than a marginal track record.

More venture capital is available today than there was last year, and there was more available last year than the year before that. Venture capital is a growth industry, and as more and more people get involved in venture capital, it begins to look more and more like the trend of the 1990s. It's becoming a glamour industry as well as growth industry, and as the amount of venture capital goes up, so does the quality of the business plans being financed. That means that this year's 11 is just that much prettier than last year's. More money attracts more competition, and more competition raises the level of the game.

It's like mile runners. These days, hundreds of mile runners are coming in with times well under four minutes, but when Roger Bannister first broke the four-minute mile, it was really an awesome thing. Mile runners are getting faster and business plan preparers are getting better.

The most valuable skill to learn when raising capital is the art of reducing risk. When I go to Las Vegas, I like to take all my chips to the roulette wheel, bet half of them on red and half of them on black and pray that zero doesn't come up. What a venture capitalist wants to see is even better odds against losing, combined with a much bigger promise of return. At the same time, it's important to remember that venture capitalists make emotional decisions. (I'm sure some of you will say that venture capitalists have no emotions, but the truth is that no decisions about money are unemotional.) Very often, the seemingly coolest decision will be made emotionally, then justified with logic.

Nine Questions Answered

1) What is the single most important aspect of the business plan, according to the venture capitalist? Management.
2) List, in chronological order, the six steps in presenting a business plan:
    a) Prospecting
    b) Approach
    c) Qualifying the source
    d) Presenting the plan
    e) Handling objection
    f) Gaining commitment

3) Name two elements of a business plan which can bring it from the 7 to 9 range up to a 10.

a) Answer the negatives.

b) Answer sheet: 2(a) It's just like...; 2(b) If it goes bad...; 2(c) The other guys have deep pockets.

4) List the five questions a venture source needs answered:

a) What business are you in?

b) How much money?

c) For what percentage of the business?

d) Who is in the deal?

e) What is unique about the deal?

5) In what order are the parts of a business plan read?

a) Characteristics of the company and industry

b) Terms of the deal

c) Balance sheet

d) Caliber of people

e) The USP (Unique Selling Proposition)

f) Once over lightly

6) Rank, in order of importance, these ten sources of linkage people for introducing your deal to venture capital sources:

a) Entrepreneur in the venture portfolio 1

b) Another venture capitalist 2

c) Accountant familiar with a venture source 6

d) Lawyer familiar with a venture source7

e) Banker familiar with a venture source 5

f) Friend of a venture source 3

g) Blind letter to a venture source 10

h) Customer of a company familiar with a venture source 8

i) Investor in a venture capitalist's portfolio 4

j) Telephone a venture source 9

7) Identify the nine members of an entrepreneurial team and highlight the most important player:

a) Partners

b) Lawyers

c) Accountants

d) Advertising Agencies

e) Consultants

f) Bankers

g) Board of directors

h) Manufacturer's agents

i) **Controller**/*V.P. Finance*

8) What should be found on the summary page of the business plan?
    a) Percentage of the company being sold
    b) Price per share vs. last price per share
    c) Minimum investment (number of investors)
    d) Total valuation (after placement)
    e) Terms of placement

9) What are the six most common debt/equity instruments available to a lender or investor?
    a) Common stock
    b) Preferred stock
    c) Debt with warrants
    d) Convertible debentures
    e) Subordinated convertible debt
    f) Straight debt

The Footwork Necessary

Now it is time to start talking about how to turn a business plan that's an 8 into a business plan that's an 11. One way of doing it is what I call "The Footwork Necessary."

How's your broken field running? Raising venture capital often parallel's trying to make a touchdown through the best defense in the league. It takes fancy footwork to work your way over that goal line.

Let's say you want to raise $250,000 for 25% of your company in a private placement. First, you must get a venture capitalist lukewarm about your situation. No one will be really enthusiastic after only one visit. I've heard that Digital Equipment Corporation (DEC), of Maynard, Massachusetts, shopped around for quite a while before American Research and Development Corporation (AR&D) finally committed itself to the tune of $70,000, an investment which, rumor has it, is worth $200 million today.

Venture capitalists see dozen of deals a day, so it will not be easy to turn them on to your proposition. Besides, they are like sheep. They'd rather follow than lead. You have to be the sheep dog to keep the pack moving.

So, once you've got the first party lukewarm, plan your strategy carefully.

One strategy that usually works begins on the second visit when you say, "I know you're not in a position to go first in this package, but I have a proposition that should interest you. I already have other investors subscribed for the first $200,000. You can have the last $50,000. You don't have to sign anything—just give me a verbal commitment contingent on my getting the other $200,000 first." If he agrees, repeat your story to anyone else who seems to be lukewarm and proceed to sell the last $50,000 five times. *You have to deal from strength.*

This is the person who will set the pace for the rest of the deal. Ask him for some sort of tentative percentages and terms and, after you've negotiated the terms, get a letter of intent for $50,000 spelling out the terms of the placement. You may have to make a few extra concessions to him, but once you have his pledge on paper or even verbally, your placement is in the bag and you should have the rest within months. Touchdown!

This example may be a little farfetched because someone has to go first. He's the one who counts, and he's the hardest one to find— not a sheep, but a true venture capitalist.

Always talk to potential investors as if your deal is all but closed, and you may have to eliminate two or three investors from the package. Never act as if you need their help or you'll be tackled before you reach midfield; rather, suggest that this one time you'll accept their money. I can't overemphasize the need to *deal from strength!*

Answering the Negative

By now, you should be able to bring your plan up from an 8 to a 9. Answering the negatives will bring it up to a 10, and 10s get financed! As I've emphasized, raising capital is not the art of selling dreams, it's the art of reducing risk. Venture capital flows in an inverse relation to the level of risk involved. So, whenever I put a business plan together, I begin by listing all the negatives. Then I answer them; first with a tape recorder, then on paper. The result should be consistent and concise descriptions of the negatives. As you plan to turn them around into opportunities, you see a problem is just an opportunity turned inside out.

Don't avoid it, don't sidestep it, and don't ignore it. Answer it head on! A great entrepreneur I worked with in Boston went bankrupt with an early company. Later, he developed a new company and went after venture capital. On the front page of his new business plan, he states that a past company of his went bankrupt. Now, rather then hemming and hawing when a venture capitalist says, "I hear you went belly up last time around," he's prepared to deal directly with the negative, and believe me, he doesn't answer by excusing his way out of responsibility: "First this conservative pension fund money fell through, then my partner was involved in a messy divorce, and that's just the beginning." Even if it's true, it sounds like sour grapes, and nobody ever raised money with sour grapes.

Instead, he practiced his answers to all the negatives, and when the question of bankruptcy comes up, he says, "You know, I did go belly up last time, but I've started five businesses, and I probably learned more from that one then from all the rest put together." One only need look at entrepreneurs like Henry Ford, Walt Disney, and Milton Hershey for prime examples of entrepreneurs who failed at least once before launching million dollar businesses. John DeLorean's biggest problem was that DeLorean Motor Cars was his first failure, and he'd already experienced too much success in the corporate world to learn how to be comfortable with failure. Sometimes earlier failures can be the biggest force behind a positive thinking entrepreneur.

To turn those 10s to 11s takes another magical element. It's nicknamed **"The Answer Sheet."** The idea is that every business plan should contain an answer sheet that summarizes the key aspect of the plan. These three examples will show you how the answer sheet works for you in your business plan:

1) It's just like...
2) The other guys have deep pockets (and long arms)
3) If it goes bad...

It's Just Like...

Example 1: Let's take a venture capitalist up in Boston who heads up the New England Venture Capital Company. We'll call him Peter.

Peter is the dean of venture capital in the New England area. He's been at it for 30 years, and he has run about $600 million in several funds over the past 20 years. His average rate of return has been 46%. He's invested in Wang Laboratories, Unitrode, and Damon Engineering, just to name a few. But the two deals he missed (both in Massachusetts) were Digital Equipment Corporation (DEC) and Data General (DG), and those are two of the biggest venture capitalist deals in history. So when Peter goes home at night, his wife says, "How are you sweetheart? Nice to see you. Did any deals come along today that look like Digital or Data General?" So if the front end of your plan looks like DEC or DG, Peter is immediately interested.

On the other hand, there's a fellow in San Francisco who invested in the early stages of Apple Computers. He runs a huge fund of venture money and is now listed in *Forbes* magazine as one of the richest people in the U.S. Let's call him Arthur.

Arthur really doesn't need money, but thousands of people made millions of dollars investing with Arthur. So when he goes out socially, his friends always pester him and ask, "Arthur, have you seen any more young Apple Computers..."

The Other Guys Have Deep Pockets (and Long Arms)

Example 2: This is a story of In-Line Technology, a company located in Bedford, Massachusetts, and run by Gene St. Onge and Hank Bok. Gene and Hank went to see a famous New York venture capitalist's Fifth Avenue apartment. During the breakfast, which lasted about two hours, the venture capitalist spent an hour and a half discussing a new painting that his wife had just purchased, then he spent a half hour discussing the business. But at the end of breakfast, the venture source agreed to put up half of the $200,000 that they were trying to raise. However, he made two conditions. The first condition was that he would not visit the company and analyze it because that alone would cost him another $25,000. The second condition was that they couldn't call him if they ran out of money. "I'm going to make a little investment with you guys and see how it works," he said, "but I can't afford to spend a lot of time with you people."

Here's where the second principle of the answer sheet means: "The other guys have deep pockets." Having a secured promise of $100,000 from a well-known venture capitalist, Gene and Hank had no problem raising the other $100,000. In fact, the deal was oversubscribed and they had to turn some money back. You see, everyone assumed that the other guy had deep pockets so the deal was safe. When the Rockefellers or General Electric back your deal, you get credibility. That helps lower-level investors (friends and relatives) sponsor your deal. Fred Smith claimed the earlier commitment from General Dynamics was crucial to launching Federal Express—because everyone knows they have deep pockets.

If It Goes Bad....

Example 3: Continuing with the story of In-Line Technologies, after about six months they did run out of money (not an uncommon experience for an entrepreneurial venture). Though they remembered the venture capitalist's instructions not to call him for help, they also knew that your best investors are your current investors. (By the way, you might want to go back and underline that sentence.) It's easily the most important in this book! So they picked up the phone and said, "Hello, Mr. Venture capitalist, this is Gene and Hank. Right, the ones who had breakfast and looked at your wife's new painting. Well, the news is that we're out of money, and we need another $200,000 to keep us going."

As you might expect, the venture capitalist wasn't quite as cavalier as he appeared when he first made the investment. Before he put up the money, he sent the business plan to a portfolio company on the West Coast where he was a director. This company needed the technology that In-Line had developed, and the venture manager and the executive vice president had both said, "Gee, this business plan looks interesting." You see, the venture capitalist had his backside well covered because one of his portfolio companies was willing, able, and even anxious to pick up the company if it ever went bad!

To make the long story short, the West Coast company flew east and bought In-Line Technologies in a 30-day period, and all of the In-Line investors wound up with a healthy profit on what turned out to be a short term investment. So the third message on the answer sheet is that there should always be a contingency plan. In other words, "If it goes bad..."

Three ways of many to create an answer sheet were just presented. But it's up to you to consider additional ways. Don't limit yourself to only these three choices. Just remember, an answer sheet is so valuable to a business plan that you only need to read it to be excited enough to invest. The plan is necessary, but the answer sheet provides the compelling motivation to be part of this deal.

You have to take a negative and make it a positive. If you try to explain it any other way, you'll get creamed, so I say, "Take your negatives and turn them around." For instance, if you're in the service business, the venture capitalist may say, "Why should I invest in a service business? Service businesses don't make money." Then you can say, "Well you've heard of Frederick Smith and Federal Express, haven't you? What's that if it's not a service business? He's delivering packages overnight; I'm delivering flowers." He then might say, "You'll never pull this deal off because of a, b, c, and d." If you're well prepared, you can turn all those negatives around, and he'll finance the deal. That's the way you turn a 9 to a 10—by answering the negatives. Now I just gave you advice that paid for this book—the Answer Sheet.

Narrowing Your Focus

When searching out a venture source, it's important that you quickly focus on locating the sources most likely to arrange capital for you. Making a thorough presentation to a venture source can be an exhausting process, so there's little point in wearing yourself out trying to sell a restaurant to someone who specializes in high-tech, or vice versa. You are selling to the wrong person. You need to locate the right person to have any hope of selling the business plan.

There are five categories of potential investors for every venture capital deal.

1) People who are familiar with your product, with you, and your industry.
2) People who are familiar and made money with you, your product, and your industry.

3) People who have made money with you, your product, and your industry and have money to invest.
4) Gap Analysis—A financial source who is overinvested in the industries he or she is most familiar with and is seeking initial investments in new industries.
5) New Boy on the Block—Dozens of new venture funds are being formed every year. Each fund has to have a first investment, and it's easier to be the first investment in a fund than to be the last.

These five categories are windows of opportunity for those seeking venture capital and while no hard statistics exist, my estimate is that the appeal of each of the five is as follows:

1) 10%
2) 25%
3) 50%
4) 10%
5) 5%

In other words, 25% of all completed venture deals would fall most closely into Category 2, while only 5% would most readily fall into Category 5; but each of these five categories of reasons to invest is equally viable to the entrepreneur beginning a search for capital.

Common Sense

When I train venture capitalists in reading business plans, what type of tricks do you think I show them to trip up unprepared entrepreneurs? Believe it or not, the best and most telling way to find out if an entrepreneur knows his or her stuff is to ask these three common sense questions. Good venture sources ask them intuitively. Please answer them below.

1) On a scale from 1 to 10, what's your business plan?

_____

2) What business are you in?

_____

3) Have you shown this plan to anyone else?

_____

_____

The answers to these questions aren't as easy as you think, so stop and think a minute before you answer. Please list your answers before you read my comments. It will make what you are about to read more useful.

1) A honest answer might be, "Hell, we've been working on this plan for three months now, and we were afraid that if we didn't get it done, we'd never get any money." Stop right there. Never tell a venture source you haven't brought the best plan you know how to write. You should always tell them it's a 10 or, if you're really confident, an 11. (If you're not overconfident, how can anyone else become convinced of its merits?)

2) When a venture source asks you what business you're in, he wants a clear, concise answer. Answers like, "I'm in the people business," or "I'm in the business of making money," or "Actually, I'm in six businesses," all side-step the question. They're cute answers for cocktail parties, but they don't raise money. An example of a crisp articulate answer might be, "We manufacture specialized equipment for a growing segment of the telecommunications industry," and go on from there. This seems like an easy question, but it's also an easy question to get tripped up on if you're not ready. Please see the last section of this chapter for a fuller account of this question.

3) This is the trickiest question of the three. If you say, "No one," it's sort of like saying, "You're the first person I've ever kissed." It's a flattering answer, but is it credible? Of course, there's a way to turn that question around to make "No one" a credible answer, and I'll get to that in a minute. The other answer is, "Yes, I showed it to so and so." Then the venture capitalist will undoubtedly respond, "Well what did so and so say?" And you will probably say, "He's thinking about it." Then the venture capitalist will probably respond (and this is the kiss of death), "If so and so says yes, then come back and we will talk." An alternate answer is, "Yes, I showed it to so and so, and he turned it down," but if you're going to give an answer like that, you're asking not to get financed. Who wants to invest in the rejects of others?

The best answer (unless the answer "no one" is actually true) is "I went to so and so for advice, and he liked the plan but said they are oversubscribed (or another credible nondestructive reason) in my industry, so he referred me to you." That's the only answer that is both credible and positive.

Your Board of Directors

The first question a venture capitalist asks when looking at a plan is "Who are the people?" The answer is easy to find. _____ is the president, _____ is the treasurer, and _____ is the controller. If their names are known, and they have good reputations, that's all to the good. But what if their names are not known? The selling job just becomes that much harder, that is, unless the venture capitalist can find a strong board of directors or consultants and investors that he or she knows. It's nice to do business with successful people who are familiar.

Very often an entrepreneur will neglect to build a board of directors. That can only hurt when it comes time for financing. A good board doesn't just happen, but if you're going to invest the time and energy (not to mention money) it takes to write a good plan, it also pays to take your time and trouble to build a good board. I seldom see a plan that's an 11 that doesn't have a great board of directors, and while a good board doesn't necessarily make a good company, it certainly won't hurt. The recognition factor of a few names on the board will go a long way toward influencing a venture capitalist to finance someone who comes without any other built-in recommendations. The same holds for consultants and investors.

Raising Capital

When Is the Best Time to Raise Capital?

The best time to sell is immediately after you've sold, and the best time to raise capital is immediately after you've raised capital—in other words, when you don't need it. This is Mancuso's Law of Small Business. The theory behind this phenomenon was developed by Dr.

Leon Festinger of Columbia University, and it's known as the theory of cognitive dissonance. Cognitive means awareness and dissonance means stress, so in other words, the theory is based on the awareness of internal stress.

Every individual who makes a difficult decision, including investment decisions, suffers from cognitive dissonance. When stress reaches an intolerable level, the individual will take action to reduce it, returning himself to a level of equilibrium—and there's no more difficult and stressful decision then whether or not to invest in a small business.

What actions does an individual take to reduce stress? Let me use the common example of the automobile buyer. Assume that you are torn between purchasing one of three mid-size cars. On a free Saturday, you go first to the Ford dealership, then across the street to the Chevy dealer, and finally down the street to the Plymouth dealer. Because you are a value conscious buyer, you compare the features and prices of each car. But after these comparisons, you are still undecided on which is the best value. After a week of pouring over all the brochures, the only thing you are sure of is you want to hurry up and get this process over with. So you finally decide to make a commitment—you go with the dealer you trust the most. For you, the whole decision making process has been difficult and stressful.

This process occurs every day and since millions of new cars are sold annually, many of us have experienced it. Everyone claims to have gotten a "Good Deal." I don't know anyone who has ever admitted to making a bad deal as a result of this process, do you?

This decision is known as a "stress decision" and the purchaser's dissonance is very high. When you bring the car home as the new owner, you take the following steps to reduce that dissonance and to justify the purchase:

1) You may inadvertently choose to leave the car in your driveway, rather then putting it in the garage. Or, you may drive it around and park it where it will be conspicuous to your peers.

2) The night you bring the car home, you will undoubtedly read the owners manual and begin to search out new information on the car you have chosen. (You will then misplace the manual and never read it again.)

3) You will become extremely receptive to television, newspaper, and magazine advertising about the car that you just purchased. The car will be the single most exciting thing in your life for a short period of time, and you will ignore all automobile ads for other cars. You will continually discover new reasons that your chosen automobile was a brilliant choice.

Because automobile companies are aware that you suffer from dissonance, they even go as far as to send a personal letter from their headquarters (usually the president) congratulating you on your wise choice. Later they will even request your help by sending you a questionnaire about the process you went through while selecting your car. There are easier and less expensive ways for automobile companies to learn this statistical information, but this questionnaire technique allows the individual to vent any residual dissonance.

The message is simple. The best time to sell is immediately after you've sold, and the best time to make a sales call is immediately after you've made a sale. In the same way, the best time to raise money is when you don't need it or you've just received money. This concept is built on Dr. Leon Festinger's theory of cognitive dissonance, and more importantly, it works.

The Entrepreneurial Model for Raising Capital (Short Version)

The process of raising capital generally requires a specific sequence of actions, I call them the "Six-Step Process." Understanding this process can really improve your chances for success. (Please also see my Seven-Step Process for Persuasion in the chapter, "How to Persuade Like an Entrepreneur.")

Step 1: Locating Sources (prospecting)
Step 2: The Approach
Step 3: Qualifying the Source
Step 4: Presenting the Business Plan
Step 5: Handling Objectives
Step 6: Gaining the Commitment

Step 1: Locating Sources (prospecting).

Without a doubt, prospecting is the hardest part of raising capital. Once you find the right person, your business plan will do most of the talking. The first step should occupy about half of the entire time used to prepare and present a business plan. Most entrepreneurs fail to do this step well and, consequently, fail at raising capital.

Step 2: The Approach.

During the approach, two things must occur. First, you should seek to reduce tension in your relationship with the venture source. While it may at times seem like an adversarial relationship, it is important to remember your goal is to make money together. Second, the entrepreneur should simultaneously be building a degree of task tension. As relationship tension is reduced, a reciprocal concern about building up the task at hand should occur. The venture source needs to invest capital, and you need to raise capital. Fulfilling your mutual needs is the task you must accomplish together.

Step 3: Qualifying the Source.

This is also known as the "Hot Button," and it focuses on the reason that the venture source will eventually wish to be included in the deal. Every situation has its salient features and attributes. Certain benefits among the features will be more important to individual capital sources than others. Not everyone invests in the same deals for the same reasons. In fact, the same plan is likely to be supported by different people for different reasons. Which button is going to be the one to press in order to raise money? What is it that source needs? These questions can only be answered through a careful study of the venture source's portfolio and needs.

Step 4: Presenting the Business Plan.

This is the step entrepreneurs handle best. They are so familiar with their product, having lived with it night and day, that they can always make a convincing presentation. The principal issue to stress in a business plan presentation is benefits.

What is the perceived value of your product vs. what
your product actually does?
What are its features?
Why will everyone need your product or service?
What will it replace?
What is it most similar to?
What will happen to your customers if they don't buy
your product or service?

Step 5: Handling Objections.

There will always be objections or attempts to postpone the
investment with the discussion of the weakness of your plan or your
product. How should you handle these objections? I suggest this very
simple technique, which I call the "Feel, Felt, Found Technique." It
works like this: When an objection is raised, don't disagree with it.
Don't be negative. Whatever you do, make sure you respond to the
objection in a sincere way. Empathize with it, legitimize it, and then
introduce new information to counter the objection.

Never counter an objection without first saying something to the
effect of, "I understand how you feel about that. In fact, you're not the
first person to bring that point up; I even felt that way initially.
However, this is not going to be a problem because..." In order to
raise capital, you must both be patient and persistent.

The first two steps are to agree with the objection, and the third
step changes his or her mind. The new information should be introduced something like this: "I'm going to show you some new information that we've just completed that should set your mind at ease."
Usually you say "we found"—remember a venture source is never
wrong. Occasionally they are only partially informed, but they are
never wrong. Your job is to have all the facts on hand so you can turn
the objection around—turn a no into a yes.

Step 6: Gaining the Commitment.

This has traditionally been viewed as the most difficult step in
raising capital, but this just isn't so. The most difficult steps are locating and qualifying the source—finding the Hot Button. If locating
and qualifying the source, the approach, and the presentation are handled properly, then gaining the commitment will be the easiest and

least stressful step in the entire process; and to gain a commitment, you may want to create an opportunity to close on an objection. To do this you must first sense what the venture sources prime objection is and then lead him to it and, by using the Feel, Felt, Found Technique, turn it around.

Frequently, an entrepreneur comes to enjoy the raising capital process so much he will talk himself right past the close. In other words, he will continue presenting the plan when he should be making the deal. Don't be afraid to close early, because one of the things a venture source is investing in is your enthusiasm. Finally, remember that raising capital is the art of reaching an agreement. It is a process of building trust and confidence. Much of an entrepreneur's skill involves being able to listen while maintaining the inner desire to perform. Mastering the art of raising capital ensures the opportunity to perform.

As a rule of thumb, you should be doing the most talking in the beginning of the Six-Step Process, asking questions, and learning. The venture source should do most of the talking near the end of the presentation. Too often, this mode of talking and listening is reversed and you are unsuccessful.

How to Write an 11 (The Long Version)

The DreamWorks business plan rates an 11 on a scale of 1-10 as it is headed by:

1) Jeffrey Katzenberg, former chairman of Walt Disney Studios—Beauty and the Beast, The Lion King, Aladdin
2) Steven Spielberg—Jurassic Park, Schindler's List, E.T.
3) David Geffen—sold his record company to MCA for billions

DreamWorks was founded in October, 1994, and has not released a film, issued a music compact disc, or landed a T.V. slot for a series. Yet, it has a line of credit for one billion dollars and a market value close to three billion dollars. It's such an exciting opportunity that the co-founder of Microsoft, Paul Allen, has invested $500,000,000 and became a part of the board of directors. He, along with other big hitters, are begging to give these entrepreneurs money. Now you have a clear picture in your mind of what it takes to write a business plan that rates an eleven on a scale of 1-10.

More than anything, raising capital is the art of success, and a venture capitalist's most important skill is the ability to recognize success in its early stages. But success is a funny thing because the people who want it are usually working so hard that they hardly notice it (at least not at first). Textron's founder, Royal Little, who was still going strong at age 91 when he addressed the CEO Clubs, attributes his success to two things: "patience and persistence." Those two traits will serve you well in the business plan process, as well. A statement I always liked about entrepreneurship is it is 1% inspiration and 99% perspiration.

The entrepreneur's job is to demonstrate his or her success in a way that a venture capitalist will appreciate it. That's why the Six-Step Process is so important. By striking just the right balance between patience and persistence, it may not make the process of raising capital any easier, but it will make it more efficient. Don't think an efficient presentation will be lost on a venture capitalist.

What follows is the long version of Mancuso's Six-Step Selling Process.

    1) Prospecting
    2) The Approach
    3) Qualifying the Source
    4) Presenting the Plan
    5) Handling Objections
    6) Gaining the Commitment

1) Prospecting

I've said it before and I'll say it again: Prospecting is the hardest part of preparing a business plan. As much as 50% of your time should be spent prospecting. One of the biggest mistakes an entrepreneur can make is to write a terrific plan and then spend his or her time showing it to the wrong venture sources. It's demoralizing, and it will just wear you down. Not only do you have to match yourself to the business, you have to match your business to your financial source.

For most entrepreneurs, this is a big revelation. When I've mentioned during seminars that an entrepreneur should spend at least three months prospecting, I've gotten looks that have said the audience thought I was crazy. "What am I supposed to do," I've been asked more than once, "Spend three months walking up and down Wall Street?" No, Wall Street has nothing to do with it. The time you spend prospecting shouldn't be spent prospecting for venture capitalists, but instead, prospecting for entrepreneurs. This is a very novel concept, but it works.

Start out by studying Stanley Pratt's *Guide to Venture Capital Sources* for the venture sources who are investing in your industry plus several of the guidebooks and directories (I like David Silver's *Who's Who in Venture Capital*). Once you have all these names and addresses, you should call or write each one you have determined would be a good potential investor and ask for a list of their portfolio of investments. For simplicity's sake, let's say you select Fred Adler (at Adler & Company) in New York. He's a technology investor, and let's say you have a software deal that you think is just right for him. The first thing you do is take a look at his prior investments. You will discover he already has investments in several software companies. Your next step is to get the names of those entrepreneurs. You then pick out the ones closest to you and start calling them. Introduce yourself and say something like, "I am an entrepreneur here in Tampa and I noticed that your operation was right up in Orlando, I'm putting together a business plan and I thought you might be able to look it over and give me a few tips. I know you've been successful in raising money, and maybe you could give me a few pointers that would help polish the plan. Do you work on Saturdays? Maybe I could drop it by Saturday morning and you could have a look at it."

You drop it off on Saturday. A week later you call him back and say, "Hi. I wonder if I could drop by next Saturday, and we can talk about the problems I'm having putting the finishing touches on my plan." Pretty soon, the entrepreneur is involved. You see, entrepreneurs love to get those kind of phone calls; they love to help each other out. And I'll tell you a secret: Everything you've heard about entrepreneurs being ornery and independent is true, but there's a certain camaraderie between entrepreneurs—a linkage.

Now you have this entrepreneur involved—one of Fred Adler's portfolio investments. He's going to see Adler periodically and he's going to mention, "A funny thing happened to me, Fred. So-and-so who works over at so-and-so came over, and I gave him a hand with his business plan. He's got a neat idea." A couple of months later when he sees him again and says, "Fred, you remember so-and-so that works over at so and so? He left so-and-so and now he's working full time on the deal." A little later, he speaks to Adler again and says, "You remember so-and-so? Well he's got a prototype finished, and its working pretty well. I think it's a pretty good deal." So Adler says, "Why don't you give me the guy's phone number?"

All of this started because you phoned the entrepreneur, and if you're smart enough, you might say something like, "I see you have a board of directors." That's usually all you have to say, and when you put your board together, he'll be one of your key linkage people.

How many people do you do this with? In my example, it only took one phone call to get the ball rolling. In reality, you may have to speak to several different entrepreneurs. As I said, this may take three or four months, but the contacts you make will be invaluable.

I'd like to say I invented this technique myself, but I didn't. The way I discovered it was by asking venture capitalists where they got their leads. More than half of their answers came from their existing portfolio companies. More than half! It's a common sense thing, but you'd be surprised how many entrepreneurs never think of it. After all, the financial source obviously has confidence in the people he invests in and trusts their judgment. Not only that, this experienced entrepreneur is multilingual. He knows how to speak your language, and he also knows how to speak that strange financial language. This is very important because you may need him to act as an interpreter.

You may ask, "Aren't entrepreneurs concerned about creating competition for themselves—especially if they're in the same field?" Well, they may be, but most of the time, they will be willing to help. Furthermore, if a business is so similar to yours that an entrepreneur turns you down, his venture capitalist wouldn't be able to do the deal anyway because in the long run, before a venture capitalist invests in the company, he clears it with portfolio companies in the same field.

The concept is to call the entrepreneur, not the venture capitalist. The venture source gets thousands of calls. You'll be somewhat unique because the entrepreneur gets much less attention. Then again, he just could be flattered to hear from you.

2) The Approach

Now you're ready for the approach. Whether you come in with an introduction from another entrepreneur or not, you will need to know the same common tips. The first tip, believe it or not, is called "Hiding the Business Plan."

Some entrepreneurs walk into an office business-plan-first. Then they lay it down on the venture capitalist's desk as though it was the Bible. The venture capitalist then picks it up, looks it over quickly, and starts off the conversation with tough, sometimes impossible questions. Before they even get a chance to get warmed up, they've blown the presentation. The venture capitalist does all the initial talking, and they are at an immediate disadvantage.

I say, keep the plan behind your back (or in your briefcase), and begin the conversation with something like, "I've looked over the investment patterns of several venture capital firms, and I think you are the logical choice for our deal because a,b,c, and d." You run off a list. This kills two birds with one stone—two big birds. First, the venture capitalist is now involved (by association) in the preparation of the document, and second, you've bypassed the tricky question, "Who else have you showed the plan to?"

By showing him or her you've done your homework, you will immediately get attention. You're not just hunting and pecking like the people who parade through his office on a regular basis. You've gotten the relationship off the ground on the right foot, and when he shows the deal to his partners, he's more likely to champion your cause.

3) Qualifying the Source

What usually happens when an entrepreneur arrives at a venture capitalist's office is that he leads with his business plan—plunks it down on the desk, and then plays dodge ball for the next hour. That's a game where you stand in the middle of a circle and they throw balls at you. Venture capitalists are experts at the game. Just when you think you've ducked and dodged every ball, they'll let you have it from out of nowhere. When you get hit on the head, they call it getting "beaned."

The problem is you can't play dodgeball with a venture capitalist for more than a few minutes. Sooner or later he's going to ask questions like, "What business are you in?" "How are you going to capture a significant market share?" and "If your company drops dead tomorrow, will the world still be OK?" These are all kinds of questions that seem simple enough, but they can get you in a lot of trouble if you're not fully prepared to handle them.

You think you've brought him the greatest thing since sliced bread, but he knows twenty ways of saying, "So what?" And he won't give you a chance to rest. Just when you think you can give him a good answer to one question, he asks you another, and another. The venture source expects every question to be answered when he asks it, and the more you think you're being bombarded, the more impatient he gets. You're thinking, "If I could just answer these one at a time, if I could just get out of this circle and they'd stop throwing balls at me, I'd be OK." So the trick is to be prepared—not just to answer his questions, but to ask some of your own. The best way to get out of the circle for a while is to put him in it. The person in control is the person asking the questions; and it's your job to be in control. So I've included a list of twelve questions you might want to use. Armed with these questions, you're going to stand up a hell of a lot better, and you're going to stand a lot better chance of finding his Hot Button. Once you've found it, you will want you push it!

Twelve Questions to Ask a Venture Capitalist

1) Ask for a list of his past investments and for the names and addresses of the entrepreneurs in his portfolio.
2) Ask about his most successful investments and the reasons for their success.
3) Ask about his most unsuccessful investments and the reasons they went bad.
4) Ask about the nature of his venture capital funds: SBIC or non-SBIC.
5) Ask about the length of the partnership maturity.
6) Ask how long he's been in business.

7) Ask about the depth of his pockets—how far he will go to support an investment.

8) Ask about the decision-making process with his firm. For some reason, those people born with deep pockets have a common genetic problem—short arms!

9) Ask about access to limited partners and his portfolio.

10) Ask him why you should deal with him.

11) Ask him about the venture firms he likes to team up with and why.

12) Ask him what type of investor he will be: Active, Passive, Leader, or Follower.

Remember, in the first interview, the venture capitalist is trying to find out what makes you tick. If you want to do business with him, you're going to want to find out what makes him tick as well. So these questions will accomplish two things. First, they'll let him know you're an inquisitive take-charge kind of person. Second, they'll help you draw him out. If, for instance, you ask him why a particular investment went bad, and he begins to list problems with genuine regret, you might want to concentrate on how your company will avoid those problems. Furthermore, you might want to solicit his advice on how to avoid other problems of that nature which might crop up. That's his Hot Button. He wants an investment that will make what he learned from his past investments pay off.

4) Presenting the Plan

When you finally do hand over your plan, the venture source will glance at it briefly and begin his or her preliminary comments. No matter how good you think your plan is, he's not going to look at it and say, "This is the greatest plan I've ever seen!" so don't go in looking for praise. It's highly likely that his remarks will be critical, and even if they aren't, they'll seem that way. Don't panic. Even if it seems like an avalanche of objections, bear in mind that Digital Equipment Corporation was turned down by everyone before American Research & Development decided to take a $70,000 chance on them. That might not seem like much now, but at the time it made all the difference. Fred Adler didn't put $25,000 into Data General until all the other established venture capitalists had turned down the deal. These are two of the best venture capital deals of all time, and they almost didn't happen, so don't expect results in the first twenty minutes.

5) Handling Objections

Raising capital is the art of reducing risks, not the art of selling dreams. It's likely that most of the objections you will hear will come in the form of questions, and most of these questions will be concerned, directly or indirectly, with reducing the level of risk. Therefore, you should answer each question carefully with the goal of reducing the risk to zero.

Here are some samples of the typical objections you might hear. "You've assembled a great team for research, but you have no controller. Smitty here has got a management background, but you really need a financial person for a controller." Or, "According to your plan, John Q. is an engineer, but you've got him set up as your marketing director." Running a small company is never easy, and raising capital is like a trial by fire. At this point, you may want to say, "Hey, we're a small company; we can't afford…"

I've even seen it happen that after the third or fourth objection, the entrepreneur says, "Hey, I don't want your money." Don't walk into a venture capitalist's office to get your ego stroked. You're there to raise money, so just be patient. As an entrepreneur, you're going to have to be part alchemist; that is, you're going to have to know how to turn lead into gold. In other words, you need to take the objection and turn it around—make it work for you. What I recommend is the Feel, Felt, Found Technique.

Feel, Felt, Found Technique

First you say, *"I understand how you feel."*

What I'm doing here is taking a sales technique that has worked for years and applying it to raise capital. What this technique does is to differentiate between the product feature and the customer benefit. For instance, every hardware store in the world sells quarter-inch drill bits, but what their customers buy are quarter-inch holes. IBM claims that its factories produce accounts receivable and payable systems, but its field sales force sells management information systems. Or, as Charles Revson, founder of Revlon cosmetics, once said, *"In our factory we make cosmetics. In the store we sell hope."* Now, I'll show you how to put this technique to work for you.

When the venture capitalist objects to John Q. as your marketing director, the first thing you should do is agree. Say something like, "I know exactly how you feel. It's very uncommon that an engineering person is also a skilled marketing person. I had the same reaction you did when my partner suggested him; but..." And here's where you supply the missing pieces of information.

I've said it before, but it's worth saying again. A venture capitalist is never wrong, he's simply not completely informed. So here's where you supply the information that puts a fix on the big picture. "...but John Q.'s been on the team for six months now, and just listen to what we found out he accomplished. He already has a purchase order from Intel, and we worked on Intel for two and a half years and came up empty. Not only that, he's written a purchase order from General Mills with advance payment-in-full. He's also instituted the first sales/cost control system in our history. He's a very methodical person, not at all flamboyant. And what we found is..." Do you get the picture? You take the objection and spin it around. That's the raising capital game. Very often a venture capitalist will challenge your plan, as much to get a chance to watch you think on your feet as to find out how a problem might be resolved.

6) Gaining the Commitment

If a venture capitalist is genuinely interested in your deal, you should be able to get him to say so. Conversely, if he's not interested, it won't do either of you any good to end the meeting with "maybe." Maybe's don't meet payrolls!

If you've done all your homework to this point—if you've boiled down the venture capital firms to the top 3 to 5 for your kind of deal—then this is really the moment of truth. You want the venture capitalist to look over your business plan, look back at you, and say, "You've got a deal." Well it doesn't happen that way. No venture capitalist is going to say "yes" at the first meeting, but if you're really lucky, he might say no. Why do I say that? Because nine times out of ten, the venture capitalist is going to say "maybe." So if you try like hell to get him to say no to the deal and he won't do it, maybe you're a step closer to being financed. Venture sources are experts at using the word maybe. It's their favorite word.

Remember, as much as you've practiced holding the business plan behind your back and saying, "Don't worry about it, it's in the plan," he's got more practice at saying "maybe." That's why the realistic thing to go for is the "no." Maybe sounds like "maybe so" to you, but it means probably not, and you don't want to hang up your deal on false hopes. Once you get the no, you can gather information for your visit to the next venture capitalist with my ten questions:

What to Do When a Venture Capitalist Turns You Down: Ten Questions

1) Confirm the Decision: "That means you do not wish to participate at this time?"
2) Sell for the Future: "Can we count you in for a second round of financing after we've completed the first?"
3) Find Out Why You Were Rejected: "Why do you choose not to participate in this deal?" (Timing? Fit? All filled up?)
4) Ask for Advice: "If you were in my position, how would you proceed?"

5) Ask for Suggestions: "Can you suggest a source who invests in this kind of deal?"
6) Get the Name: "Whom should I speak to when I'm there?"
7) Find Out Why: "Why do you suggest this firm, and why do you think this is the best person to speak to there?"
8) Work on an Introduction: "Who would be the best person to introduce me?"
9) Develop a Reasonable Excuse: "Can I tell him that your decision to turn us down was based on_____?"
10) Know Your Referral: "What will you tell him when he calls?"

Armed with the information you've gathered at your first meeting, you should go into the next venture capitalist's office with the same intention: to get a "no." You go through the whole song and dance again (maybe with a little more polish this time), and you go for the "no," and it may be a little harder to get this time. The point is that you're probably not there to get money for next year; you want it next month or next week. "Maybe" means, "Maybe I'll tell you 'no' next month."

You visit your three or four most likely venture capitalists, and if you can't get them to say, "No, we don't want the deal," then it becomes a waiting game. Chances are that if they are going to finance you, they won't hang you up as long so that they endanger the company. If they're not... well, that's why you've tried to get the no's. If your best bets turn down the deal, there's probably something wrong with it. Then you're back to the drawing board. Maybe it's your plan, maybe it's your people, or maybe it's your product. Try to find out what they don't like about it, then rework it and bring it back. Don't start picking out venture capitalist firms at random, trying to sell them the plan that you couldn't sell your best bets, because it's just going to mean more time and more frustration. If your best bets don't want the deal, then 999,999 chances out of a million, the firms that you've already ruled out won't want them either.

What do you do? If you really believe in your plan and you need money right away, you may have to go for debt. If you can wait, you go back and work on your plan some more. You use everything you've learned from everyone you've talked to, and you try to make it that much better. Those are my suggestions on what to do if you don't get financed (and not everybody will) When you do get financed—and my technique has raised hundreds of millions of dollars—then the hard work begins.

Remember, only the best business plans (10s and 11s) raise venture capital. The others raise capital that has to be paid back (debt) or must be internally generated. Before I conclude this chapter, I want to offer more advice on how to answer the question, "What business am I in?" As I said before, it's one of three critical questions a venture capitalist will ask. So here is a little help.

What Business Am I In?

How to Establish Corporate Strategy

No one knows for sure what makes one corporate strategy work and others fail. It is known that those companies that succeed have better strategies than those that fail. It's not known whether the strategy causes success or the success results in the strategy. Consequently, it is difficult to offer reliable advice about setting corporate strategy in a winning entrepreneurial venture. More practical advice is possible about ineffective strategies.

While setting strategy, the leader must assimilate the many variables that interact simultaneously while developing a strategy. Strategy is a function reserved only for the chief executive officer of a small company. The top person is the lead dog in the sled pack, and he exchanges an unobtrusive view of what's in front of him for a willingness to establish the course.

A computer will never lose in competition against the world's greatest checker player—it will at least draw with the most talented checker-playing human beings. In other words, the computer has the capacity to assimilate the finite number of moves in a checker game, and it is programmed to always win or at least draw. It can never lose. The best a human can achieve against a computer in checkers is a draw. This is not so in the more complex game of chess.

A master chess player can beat most computers fairly consistently—not an average chess player, mind you, but a master chess player. The reason most computers cannot outthink a chess player is twofold: The computer can't handle within its memory the capacity a human being can handle within its memory. In other words, a person's brain can store and access more data of a useful nature than the computer's memory. Also, a computer must handle decisions on a step-by-step incremental or digital basis, whereas an individual can decide upon a strategy that encompasses a wide range or series of moves (analog), and the master chess player can beat the computer in most games.

Effective management of a small business requires a clear and concise answer to the question, "What business are you in?" This single question has been most difficult to resolve for all businesspeople, for small as well as large businesses. The answer is elusive, and the pace of internal or external changes in a small enterprise requires an endless examination of this question. This question is the full-time focus of most presidents and executives. Its answer is the zenith of intellectual achievement for any leader or chief executive officer. All but a handful of leaders answer it ineffectively and thereby fail at this most fundamental level of conceptualizing. According to Mr. Peter Drucker, a management expert, all companies that answer this question properly eventually succeed.

"What business am I in?" is the question that establishes the mission of any organization. An effective answer requires a definite, accurate, meaningful statement of an organization's goals, objectives, and purposes. The question is bit circular and jellylike, but it lies at the heart of leadership-related activities in a profit-seeking business. A complete answer requires a comprehensive analysis of the strengths and weaknesses of the firm, combined with the appreciation of the firm's future needs within a changing marketplace. This issue was originally articulated by Peter Drucker in the mid-fifties in his classic book, *The Practice of Management*, and has become one of the most popular subjects for modern management

While "What business am I in?" might also be a casual thought for a lost shopper, it has another more crucial focus. The answer to this central question separates good from bad management. It's a circular question that never ends, much like the individual's counterpart, "Who am I?" The strategy of selecting the right business to be in is only part of the right answer. Being a success requires more. The right answer must be followed up with winning tactics and execution to achieve management success. Tactics and strategy must interplay to properly answer the question, "What business am I in?"

Comparing *tactics* with *strategy*, it can be said the strategy employed determines whether one wins or loses a war. The tactics are for a single battle, not necessarily the war. Definition from *Webster's New Collegiate Dictionary:*

STRATEGY: From the Greek, meaning *generalship*; The science and art of employing the political, economic, psychological, and military forces of a nation or a group of nations to afford the maximum support to adopted policies in peace or war. The science and art of military command exercised to meet the enemy in combat under advantageous conditions. A careful plan or method. The art of devising plans toward a goal.

This last statement in the definition about goals best suits our purpose. It relates well to running entrepreneurial ventures. Now, in Webster's definition of tactics, we find that again it is a word derived from the Greek.

TACTICS: The art and science of disposing and maneuvering forces in combat. The art and science of employing available means to accomplish an end. A system or mode of procedure.

Notice how tactics differ from strategies.

The objectives of all dedicated employees should be to analyze all situations thoroughly, anticipate all problems prior to their occurrence, have answers for these problems, and move swiftly to solve these problems when called upon. However, when you are up to your ass in alligators, it is difficult to remind yourself that your initial objective was to drain the swamp.

Notice the difference between strategies and tactics in this often-quoted phrase. It's catchy the way they interrelate in the story because each individual can relate to the story of draining the swamp, which is the long-term objective. But the alligators of life tend to get in the way. That's why some entrepreneurs are successful, and some are not.

In the year 378, the Roman Emperor Valens and 40,000 Roman Legionnaires were slain in battle by an inferior force of Goths led by Fritigem. On the fields of Mars near Adrianople, these Romans fell victim to an opponent who developed and implemented a superior plan of battle. The demise of the empire was foretold as adversaries began outfoxing and outfighting the heretofore immovable Romans.

The consequences of mismanagement for presidents of small companies can be equally disastrous. A poorly managed small company can actually cease to exist if it performs poorly, whereas its larger competitors do not face such frightening consequences. Without a doubt, the issues that separate success and failure for small companies focus on small business strategy.

Examples

Lets look at some "for instances" on the same basis. How about soft drinks? In the late 1920s, the leading manufacturer for soft drinks was a Boston-based company known as Moxie. They had a larger market share than Coca-Cola. Moxie determined their critical skill to be marketing herb-like soft drinks. Coca-Cola determined their critical skill to be supplying a variety of soft drinks, not unusual herb-like drinks. Today, Moxie has moved its business south and is still selling a few million dollars worth of its unusual drink, while Coca-Cola is an international giant. Why couldn't Moxie capture that market before Coca-Cola even had the chance to get off the ground? Why didn't they properly answer the elusive question, "What business am I in?"

"The problem with the railroad industry is that it defined its mission too narrowly," claims Professor Theodore Leavitt of the Harvard Business School. Rather than answering the popular question, "What business am I in?" by the single word, "railroad," a sounder strategic choice would have been built around the phrase, "the transportation industry." What has placed the railroads in trouble is their narrow view of the business they're in. The railroad business, per se, offered a rather bleak future. In turn, the transportation industry (which encompasses all modes of transportation) offered a much brighter future.

The same issue, although not articulated by Dr. Leavitt in the article, can be highlighted in other industries that have failed in strategic decisions. Another is the U.S. typewriter industry in the early mid-fifties. It defined its business by the machine and by its corporate name as well, such as Royal *Typewriter*, Underwood *Typewriter*, Olivetti *Typewriter*. They undoubtedly would answer the question, "What business am I in?" with the single word, "typewriter." Notice the parallel with the railroad industry? Both had the narrow interpretation of their business spelled out in their name—*Typewriter* and *Railroad.*

Yet if they had chosen the broader interpretation in response to the same query, they would have offered the phrase, "We are in the office equipment business." In fact, they might even had said, "We are in the international business machine business." It's interesting in hindsight to examine the sales success of the large dominant supplier today in the international business machine business, which, if you're unaware, is known as IBM. The sales of IBM today dwarf the sales of the entire typewriter industry. However, in the early 1950s this was not the case.

How to establish corporate strategy is as elusive as finding a needle on a sandy beach. It just seems to slip through your fingers.

A business's success in the marketplace depends on total commitment to marketing—on whether the organization is entirely imbued with the marketing concept or whether it views its marketing as an entity separate and independent of the other divisions. Commitment to a marketing orientation must permeate the organizational whole, from the very top through every major division.

Too often, the concept of marketing has been limited to the sole endeavor of selling. Though selling is an integral part of total marketing, it does not encompass the whole of the marketing concept. The essence of marketing in an entrepreneurial venture is evidenced in five major areas of endeavor. To fulfill and utilize the marketing concept to serve the needs of the company and, in turn, increase the sales of the company, a marketing organization must be willing to do the following:

1) Define its market areas.
2) Research customer needs and wants.
3) Develop and redevelop product and/or service to meet the demand.

4) Recruit, select, and train employees to develop the product or service.
5) Develop its sales approach and advertising support.

A person seldom begins a journey unless he first knows his desired destination. If he is a careful traveler, he has planned his route, his stops, his time of arrival, and how much it will cost to get there. If you don't know where you are going, any road will take you there. The lead dog in a sled dog pack exchanges an unobtrusive view for willingness to set the course. When the lead dog has marketing orientation, the sled dog pack can run swiftly to its destination.

A business plan answers the question of what business you are in concisely and accurately, and, like the shepherd leading the flock, it provides a silhouette against the skyline for all the sheep to follow.

Corporate Checklist for a Business Plan

A. The formation of a corporation constitutes the formation of a separate legal entity under state law. It is essential that the services of a competent local attorney be obtained to help the client file the Articles of Incorporation and meet the terms of the state law.

B. An election for the corporation to be treated as a Section 1244 small business corporation. Discuss with your attorney if applicable.

C. Following is a list of steps that will be necessary for a new corporation. It should not be deemed to be all-inclusive. It is not intended to be used as a substitution for a competent attorney.

1) **Incorporators**—Have a meeting of the incorporators and determine the following:
   a) The corporate name
   b) The classes and number of shares to authorize
   c) Business purpose for which the corporation is formed
   d) Initial capital needed
   e) Determine the directors
   f) Location of business
   g) Determine corporation officers and salaries
   h) Check on thin incorporation

2) **Determine Start-Up Date**—If the corporation is to take over a going business, a start-up date should be set at some time in the future so that all steps can be taken without unnecessary haste.

3) **Corporate Name**—Check at once with the Secretary of State to see if the corporate name is available.

4) **Notify the following:**
   a) **Insurance Company**—have policies changed. May also be necessary to increase coverage.
   b) **Creditors**—inform all creditors of former business.
   c) **Customers**—inform all customers of former business.

d) **State and local authorities,** such as state unemployment and disability department and country assessor.

5) **Transfer of Assets and Liabilities**—If the corporation is to take over a going business, determine what assets and liabilities are to be turned over to the corporation, and if shares or notes are to be issued in exchange. Does it qualify as a tax-free exchange under IRC Section 3?

6) **Banks**—Select bank or banks and furnish resolution authorizing who is to sign checks and negotiate loans.

7) **Identification Number**—File application for an Identification No. Federal Form SS-4.

8) **Workmen's Compensation**—File for coverage.

9) **Unemployment Insurance**—File for coverage.

10) **Special Licenses**—Check on transfer of new license such as food, drug, cigarette, liquor, etc.

11) **Final Returns**—If the new corporation is taking over a going business, file Sales Tax, FICA Tax, Unemployment Tax, and Workmen's Compensation final returns for the old business after the corporation takes over the operation of the new business.

12) **Federal Unemployment**—Determine if final Form 940, Employer's Annual Federal Unemployment Tax return is to be filed on old business.

13) **Sales Tax**—Obtain a new sales tax vendor's license on the first day of business. Do not use any tax stamps purchased by the former business or do not use the plate from the former business.

14) **Tax Election:**

a) **Election under Subchapter S**—Determine if the corporation is going to elect to be taxed as a partnership under Subchapter S. If so, prepare and file Form 2553, Election by Small Business Corporation, within thirty days after the first day of the fiscal year or date new corporation commences to "do business."

b) **Section 1244 Stock**—If corporation is eligible, issue stock in accordance with a written plan included in the minute.

c) **Year Ending**—Determine the date the corporation's year will end.

d) **Accounting**—Determine the method of accounting the corporation will use.

Chapter 3

Bank Loans

How to Think Like a Banker

As an entrepreneur, when you go to your banker's office to request a loan, it is your duty to be thoroughly prepared to show them that a loan to you is a low-risk proposition because every banker has been burned at some point in their career, and no banker wants to experience that pain again. Be prepared to answer every doubtful question he or she has. You've learned a lot so far about bankers as people—the way they think, the way they tend to act. Now use that information to improve your negotiating abilities. This combination of information and preparation is the most powerful negotiating tool in the world.

Bankers don't want to make high-risk loans regardless of the profit prospects for your business. They are bankers, not venture capitalists. Bank lending is the process by which someone lets you borrow money and expects you to be paid back with interest. It is not an equity process. There is no "upside." Even if you turn your high-risk business into an immensely profitable one, all your banker gets out of it is principal and interest. Bankers prefer to lend to low-risk, low-profit ventures than to high-risk businesses with exciting profit prospects because they want their money back. Avoiding failure earns your banker a promotion, not hitting a home run!

Bankers often resemble turkeys because of the way they flock. But, they also resemble elephants: they have very long memories. You can go to your banker's office confident about your strong, healthy business, but if he remembers that six years ago you had to sign personally for a loan, he'll want you to sign again. "But I paid that loan off perfectly on schedule," you protest. "Doesn't that count for something?" Most small business borrowers do, in fact, pay their loans back conscientiously, so you really don't distinguish yourself from the crowd by doing so. I strongly suggest borrowing and paying back a loan when you don't need it, just to establish credibility. You've proven you're a good customer of the bank, but you have to prove you're the best customer to get off personal loan guarantees.

How to Answer Crucial Questions Your Banker Will Ask

You can distinguish yourself by being prepared. I think you'll be surprised to learn that a thoroughly prepared borrower has a four times greater chance of having his or her loan approved than a borrower who waltzes into the bank without knowing the answers to the questions. That's a significant advantage.

You should know the answers to the following five questions. Your banker will ask them, and you should have the answers on the tip of your tongue.

What a Banker Wants to Know about Your Loan Request

1) How much money do you need?
2) How long do you need it for?
3) What are you going to do with it?
4) When and how will you repay it?
5) What will you do if you don't get the loan?

You know how much money you need, and you would probably love to keep it for ten years, but most commercial banks have a policy of lending for less than twelve months. A banker usually feels comfortable offering a maximum maturity of 90 days to a small business owner, but you can get a six-month loan. My advice is to ask for a six-month loan with an automatic renewal to be given by the bank if all conditions remain satisfactory, i.e., if you make prompt payments and the bank is happy with the interest structure. In this way, you secure for yourself a loan of one year, which is the longest loan you can possibly get from a bank today.

Two Elements a Banker Relies on for Repayment of a Loan

1) Collateral
2) Cash flow generated by the business (pays the loan 99% of the time)

Ninety-nine percent of small business loans are repaid from cash flow generated by the business. Please reread that sentence—it's important, thank you! Your business plan should clearly show how you plan to generate enough cash to pay back the loan. Your banker will still want collateral. He'll want to know the worth of the assets of your business. If he says your assets aren't enough, and he wants your summer home and your spouse's car, you might remind him that more collateral does not turn a bad loan into a good loan. A good loan is paid back from the cash flow of the business. So when your banker talks about collateral, you should talk about cash flow! Remind him that 99% of loans are paid out of cash flow, and show him your strong cash flow. Whenever he says "collateral," you respond by saying "cash flow."

Four Ways You Actually Repay a Loan

1) Cash flow generated by the business (99% of the time)
2) Get an investor (equity infusion pays off some debt)
3) Sell an asset or the business
4) Borrow somewhere else

Two Reasons for Renewing a Loan

1) It didn't happen!
2) It happened, but you used the money for something else

Many entrepreneurs have renewed a loan for one of the two reasons mentioned above. We get stuck with frequent renewals that we constantly have to explain to our banker ("It didn't happen because....") or "I used the money for something else because...."). If you are constantly in your banker's office to renew your 90-day note because the time frame is too short, you will constantly be giving him excuses that make you look bad. Within 90 days, it's pretty unlikely that your business is going to "happen" in such a big way that you're not going to need to renew the note. Also, it's pretty likely that a more pressing need (for example, payroll) than the one for which you told him you needed the money will come up. For an entrepreneur, this is just part of running a business. You have to be flexible, so you do what you have to do. Bankers don't admire flexibility, and they hate surprises. For bankers, there is no such thing as good news *and* bad news. There is only good news and better news. That's why I talked earlier about going for a six-month loan with an automatic renewal if all conditions remain satisfactory. That's a good option; it avoids surprises.

What If He's Just Plain Mean?

A doctor comes into a heart transplant patient's room to tell him about the available heart donors.

> "We've got three donors for you," the doctor says, "a 36-year-old steamfitter—real healthy guy, a 46-year-old marathon runner, and a 56-year-old banker." Which heart do you think the patient decides to take a chance on?
>
> The patient says, "I'll take the banker's heart."
>
> The doctor, astonished, says, "Why do you want the oldest heart when you could have these younger, much healthier hearts?"
>
> The patient answers, "Because I know that the banker's heart has never been used!"

Many entrepreneurs can relate to that story, but, as I've stressed from the beginning, your banker is the key to the growth of your business, and your relationship with him or her should be a friendly and helpful one.

But what if you've really tried to get along with your banker and the relationship is just not working? You feel that your requests for a loan are being arbitrarily turned down. Should you go over his head?

Probably not, because even if you do, it is likely that the same banker will sit on your loan committee or be contacted by the new loan officer. You'll be in negotiations with a banker you made look bad. This is not a win-win negotiating situation, it's a win-lose situation, and guess who is going to lose—the person with the money or the person with the idea? Mancuso's Golden Rule is, "Those that have the gold make the rules." The person with the idea is going to lose.

My advice to you is to get another banker at another bank. If you really have a personality conflict with your banker, don't borrow money from his bank. He may decide to make trouble for you at every turn. That advice is 99 percent infallible, so take note.

If you're very happy with your bank, but not your banker, and don't want to change banks in order to change bankers, try speaking with your banker's boss. Politely request to change to a different banker. Be prepared to describe the problem as simply "poor communication" and take most of the blame yourself. Do not attempt to crucify your banker. His boss will know what you are getting at and will appreciate your tact. You will get what you wanted—a different banker—without alienating a possible member of your loan committee. Generally, though, never pick a bank, always pick a banker. The individual you work with is usually more important than the institution you choose.

If you do decide to change bankers and banks, there are a couple of good ways to improve your position. The best way to find a good banker is to ask for a referral from a successful entrepreneur. (Bankers tell me that the nicest thing a customer can do for them is to offer a good referral; in fact, the single best thing you can do for your banker is to refer a good depositor.) This is probably the most valuable piece of information in this book. You see, most entrepreneurs approach a bank directly. They try to determine who they should talk to about a loan by asking the first bank employee they meet for a recommendation. Everyone who applies for employment at a bank must take an IQ test, and the people who score the lowest man the front desks or the phones at the bank.

Entrepreneurs are natural phone people—we do our best wheeling and dealing on the phone. We make the mistake of approaching a banker the way we would another entrepreneur—on the phone. Bankers hate phones. Phones make them feel insecure. They like to write letters and send memos. They like communications they can file. You may hate to pin yourself down by putting all your communications with your banker in writing, but that's too bad. You're in the business of becoming your banker's best friend, and that includes humoring his formal tendencies. Choose a banker who was recommended to you by a successful entrepreneur and approach him or her in writing. Don't phone!

Ten Tips for Communicating Effectively with Banks

1) When calling a bank, it's always best to ask for the president's office. Unlike small companies, banks always seem to put their lowest-level employees on the phones. But the secretary in the president's office is always knowledgeable and can actually answer questions.

2) Banks will generally lose your call, and about one call in four always seems to result in being cut off. Your call will always be transferred at least twice—the average is about four times. (One of our calls was actually transferred twelve times.) Also, the bigger the bank, the longer you'll spend on hold.

3) Never call and say you want to send a letter of complaint to the bank. Most large banks have a person in charge of complaints, and your phone calls or letters produce fewer results when you write to the complaint person. Complaints should be sent to the president, with copies to others, to have any hope for results.

4) Trying to locate a commercial loan officer is very difficult in most banks. Calling a branch to find out who to approach for a commercial loan is much less effective than calling the president's office to ask the same question.

5) Banks change loan officers and organizational charts about as frequently as O'Hare Airport changes air traffic

controllers. Consequently, the bank telephone directory, if you happen to have one, is always out of date and is effectively useless. Throw it away.

6) A bank's personnel department is totally useless for finding out who to speak to on any subject. Don't waste your time calling them.

7) Letters are always better than phone calls because banks will eventually forward letters to the appropriate people. And while phone calls are frequently cut off, letters are almost never thrown away. Letters work well, but responses take weeks. Plan ahead.

8) Letters sent to bank employees are most effective when they are sent to several people. It is better to send a letter and follow it up with a phone call than it is to call blind. The most effective letter-writing technique is to get copies to people at the branch, the asset lending group, the main office, and the loan department because these people seldom talk to one another, and the copies force them to talk a little.

9) A referral from a good customer of the bank is invaluable. If you say on the phone or by letter, "So-and-so referred me," it puts you into a new category. The best way to approach a bank is through a customer referral.

10) Loan officers don't get promoted for the loans they make (or don't make). They get promoted for the deposits they bring the bank. It is, therefore, better to talk or write about deposits, not loans. The nicest favor you can do for a bank or a banker is to refer a good depositor to the bank. It's invaluable.

11) While I promised you only ten points, I couldn't resist this bonus point. The average salary of the average commercial loan officer is about $60,000 annually. These lesser-paid people are making decisions about the well-being of your multimillion-dollar business. Your lifestyle may be significantly different from theirs, and it must be factored into your relationship.

How to Stay off Personal Loan Guarantees (and get off them if you're already on)

Is It Worth It to You?

If you've followed the strategy mapped out so far, you are well on your way to becoming the best customer your banker ever had, but you probably worry about personal loan guarantees. By a personal loan guarantee I mean any form of loan under which, if your business is unable to make the payments, you, as its guarantor, are personally responsible for doing so.

Bankers, being the orderly people they are, like to do a two-step negotiation—first the loan and then the guarantee. After the loan is negotiated, they like to say, "By the way, with all loans we require borrowers to fill out these personal financial statements." You should seek a one-step negotiation with the guarantee negotiated as part of the loan application. When your banker says, "I'm sorry, that's not negotiable," you should say innocently, "Gosh, isn't everything negotiable?"

Think of the negotiation process as a pyramid, and the tip is the personal loan guarantee.

If you are currently on a personal loan guarantee, write down how much it would be worth to you to get off the personal loan guarantee. Do this before you begin negotiating. When negotiating such a sensitive issue, you don't want to win the battle just to find out that you've lost the war.

1) Write a dollar amount.
2) Consider interest rates. Would you pay a higher rate if you didn't have to sign personally for the loan?
3) Would you be willing to borrow less money in exchange for not having to sign a personal guarantee?
4) Would you be willing to put up a higher compensating balance for the money you've borrowed?
5) Would you settle for a shorter maturity on your loan?

This step is crucial because it will prevent you from allowing the banker to take advantage of your emotional desire to get off the personal loan guarantee. Over time, personal loan guarantees have become an emotional issue between entrepreneurs and lenders: Entrepreneurs today are overzealous about their value and the need to get off the guarantees.

Between you and me, I have been on a few personal guarantees. In a few select cases, when it came down to getting the money but not getting off the personal loan guarantee, I took the money because the money was doing me enough good to offset the potential harm of the guarantee.

Set limits for yourself before negotiations begin. Know how much it is really worth to you (and to your spouse) to get off the personal loan guarantee before you step into the banker's office for negotiations. When it gets to the short strokes, the value of getting off personal loan guarantees suddenly gets bigger and bigger, and you end up losing everything.

At first glance, a higher compensating balance might seem to be the most painless offer to make for release from a personal loan guarantee. After all, you have to keep your cash somewhere. Why not keep it at the bank in the form of a compensating balance? Your banker will encourage you to do this. Bankers love compensating balances because, as a rule of thumb, banks only have a capital base of 5 percent. This means that they can take your compensating balance of, say, $150 and potentially turn it into $3,000 (20 x $150) in interest-earning loans. By now you're probably thinking, *"Compensating balances won't cost me anything—after all, I've got to keep some cash at the bank anyway, and it'll make my banker happy."*

This reasoning is problematic because it overlooks one thing: Compensating balances raise the actual rate of interest on your loan. It works like this: You borrow $1,000 from the bank at 12 percent interest, but you are asked to leave $150 in the bank as a compensating balance. This seems relatively painless because it leaves you with $850 to use. Your actual rate of interest now, though, is not 12 percent. It is 12 percent divided by .85, or 14.1 percent. If you are not willing to pay that rate of interest, do not agree to leave that compensating balance. If 14 percent is a better interest rate than the banker is willing to offer if you don't leave a compensating balance then, of course, you'll want to reconsider.

Understanding the role of compensating balances and idle balances is part of cash management, a subject too large to be covered in this book. I would like you to note, though, that a study by the Caruth Institute of Owner-Managed Business at Southern Methodist University in Dallas, Texas, showed that a major bank's pretax earnings on small business loans were 2.7 percentage points higher than its earnings on loans to large firms, in spite of the higher administrative costs and the greater risks of small business loans.

This finding indicates that the small businesses were paying an average of 17.7 percent interest instead of the 15.0 percent interest averaged by large businesses.

The study revealed further that the reason for this was that small businesses did not manage their idle cash as well as the large firms did. They left more of their funds in idle cash balances that the bank could lend. If your financial officer and accountant are not well versed in cash management, you may have a weak catcher and center fielder.

Ask and Ye Shall Receive

The next important step is simply to ask to get off the personal loan guarantee and to keep asking until you get closer to your goal.

To get out of your personal loan guarantee pickle, you are also going to have to ask a sequence of questions.

First, ask your banker if everybody who borrows from her bank signs personally for corporate debt. If she says yes, say,

"Come on, I'm sure some of the bigger companies don't sign." Find out how "big" you have to be to avoid signing. You want to know where your bank draws the line. You should also seek out small business owners who are borrowing without personal guarantees. Determine what they have that you don't have and keep in mind the arguments about public companies and Lee Iacocca that I present later in this section. Second, ask your banker, politely, what those larger businesses have that you don't have in terms of ability to pay back their loans.

By now your banker will have asked you the big guilt question:

"Why don't you want to sign personally? Aren't you going to pay back the loan?" Bankers practice this question in front of their mirrors at home. They love how it puts you on the spot. You should practice your answer to it just as often.

Throw her a curve with this answer:

"Of course, I'm going to pay it back, Joan. You've seen my business plan, the loan is well accounted for. Besides, I've paid back all my other loans, but this isn't that simple. Life is more complicated than sets of numbers would have us believe. It may not be all that logical, but for me this is a big issue. I lose sleep over it. It's like my wife, Matilda, was saying the other day. She asked me why we couldn't just pay off the mortgage on our beautiful quarter-million-dollar house in Cape Cod. I explained to her that the 6 percent interest on the mortgage is the least expensive borrowed money we've got and that it would be foolish to pay it off. Do you know what she told me? She said, 'I know the numbers and the facts, but I've always wanted to live in a house that was all mine, with no mortgage.' You know, Joan, I guess I feel the same way about the personal loan guarantee. The loan will be paid back with or without the guarantee, but I'll sure sleep better without it. I'll even perform better at work without the extra worry, and we both want me to perform at my best, don't we? Joan, can you relate to my wife's feeling?"

Give your banker this second reason:

"With the present turmoil in the banking industry, I am very uneasy about personally guaranteeing corporate debt because that decreases my flexibility. If your bank gets in trouble, like Bank of America, Bank of New England, Continental Illinois, or Republic did, the personal guarantee could hinder my flexibility while the regulators are undoing the mess at your bank. My only choice in such a predicament might be to borrow elsewhere personally for my business. The guarantee would prevent me from being able to keep my business going. I think you'll agree that in these times bank failure is not a remote possibility, and that it's unhealthy for both of us to put a ball and chain around the foot of the one person who could bail out the company if the bank gets in trouble."

Now you can see why you've laid such careful groundwork for a warm, friendly relationship with your banker. You want her to understand how you feel about signing that loan guarantee, not just to look at the numbers. When she throws you that hard logical question, you can use it as a launching pad for your own "Matilda" story. Then you can get logical again by telling her that, quite frankly, the worry over the guarantee is adversely affecting your performance.

Ask for the Future, Not for Now

A person's willingness to do something for you depends not only on what you are asking for, but also on how much lead time you are giving her.

For example, a representative from your alma mater calls you on Friday and asks if you'll participate in a telephone fundraising drive on Monday. Chances are you'll beg off. But what if the same person calls you on Friday and asks if you might be willing to help out with the fundraising drive coming up in a couple of months. You'll probably say yes or maybe—not no. Use your understanding of this human tendency to say yes to future commitments on your banker. Her willingness to do something for you is partially a function of the amount of time you give her to do it. If you come in close and tight about wanting to get off the guarantee next week, she won't do it.

Try this approach:

"On my $100,000 loan, of which I've paid back $50,000, would it be unreasonable for me to ask if I could be released from the personal loan guarantee when I've paid back $75,000? I know I'll sleep better." If she says no, ask her, "If I came in here after I'd paid off $99,990 of that loan, and I told you that the personal guarantee was still causing me sleepless nights, wouldn't you let me off the guarantee?" Of course she'll say, "I don't see why not," and then you've got something to work with. At least you've established in your banker's mind the possibility of letting you off the guarantee. The best way to get off a personal loan guarantee is to ask and to continue to ask and bargain after you have shown some sign of your ability to pay back the loan. Ask for the future, not for now. It may be a slow and tedious process, and it is even possible that your banker won't let you off until you've paid off nine-tenths of the loan, but remember that you are taking on the enormous task of reprogramming her elephant-like memory. That memory will work in your favor on the next loan, when she remembers that letting you off the personal guarantee did not ruin her career.

Help Your Banker Be a Hero—
Give Her a Story

What if you have no track record of previous loans to show your banker? All is not lost. Not having a track record is better than having a bad track record, and you can make your case stronger with a good story. A good story can be even better than an average track record.

It's your job to provide your banker with a very neatly bundled, coherent, exciting, and colorful story. Your banker would love to go home to her husband and tell him how she single-handedly saved your terrific new company and made the world a better place.

She would be even happier to have a wonderful story to tell to the loan committee. Remember, your banker will have to go to the loan committee with your request to be released from the personal loan guarantee. She would much rather go to the loan committee with a wonderful story than with just a loan guarantee release request.

Let's say your company is producing a newly invented monitoring device for babies that will eliminate crib deaths—Sudden Infant Death Syndrome (SIDS). Do you go into your banker's office and ask her for a loan for the production of an electronic oscilloscope? No! You tell her the story of how her loan to you will protect the children of the community. Make the banker a hero for lending you the money.

It's your responsibility as an entrepreneur to do that for your banker. Maybe you'll even get her promoted. Don't forget to take her to lunch or to a ball game because she's your company's best friend. You'll have a great time, and eventually the efforts you've put in to be her best customer will pay off, and her need for your personal loan guarantee will be a thing of the past.

Ask for Money When You Don't Need It

Since we're talking about timing, I'd like to reintroduce at this point Mancuso's Law: The only time to raise capital is when you don't need it. Banks prefer to lend money to borrowers who have borrowed at least once and have paid back at least one loan on time. It's a psychological factor, just as they prefer to lend to a business that already has an account at their bank. Take advantage of your banker's methodical nature. Remember all those audit trail letters in your file? Bankers remember everything; they're like elephants with file cabinets instead of trunks.

Bankers like to hear from you frequently because it makes them feel more secure about their loan to you. I recommend monthly payments on a loan over payment every six months. Get in the habit of keeping your banker up-to-date on your business.

If you expect to need to request a new loan in six months, mention to your banker now that you are working on an exciting expansion that might require more credit. When you actually make your request three months later, she will be pleased. It will confirm her expectations and your reliability. If, on the other hand, you just walk in and tell her that you are out of money and need more for expansion, she will treat what is basically an identical request with suspicion and mistrust.

Don't forget to invite your banker to your facilities to see the results of your latest loan. Bankers love an excuse to get out of their offices, and they need to fully understand your business and see it in operation to be totally comfortable.

If You Can't Get off It, Chip at It

You can chip away at the personal loan guarantee at several negotiation points if asking to get off doesn't work. Don't give up just because the banker didn't give in after a couple of tries. No banker likes to give up personal loan guarantees. Start chipping away at the guarantee by negotiating with your banker about different aspects of it. First, let's talk about the form of the guarantee. There are two basic types of guarantees:

1) Joint and several
2) Payment versus collection (indemnity versus guarantee)

Are you guaranteeing the payment of the debt or the collection of the debt? In other words, if the business fails, can the bank sue you and the business simultaneously and proceed against both entities aggressively until it gets paid (joint and several guarantee) or does it have to sue the business first and, if it fails to get the money from the business, then go after you (payment versus collection guarantee)? The bank would obviously prefer the joint and several guarantee. It would rather sue both you and the company simultaneously rather than have to wait until it finds out it can't get the money from the company to go after you. This is a negotiating point. If you can get an indemnification guarantee instead of a joint and several guarantee, you are one step closer to establishing yourself as a customer who does not sign personal guarantees. Just knowing that there are different kinds of guarantees will help you to negotiate. For example, you could give up your push for an indemnification guarantee late in the negotiations and ask your banker to give up something in return. These are legal points, and I certainly advise you to consult with your lawyer, but I frown on letting your lawyer negotiate for you. Do it yourself, even though you'll probably have to consult your lawyer continuously during the negotiations.

There is a second negotiating point concerning the form of the guarantee. If your company has multiple stockholders, you can negotiate for limited guarantees. Try to share the personal guarantee liability with the other major stockholders of your company. For example, if you have five equal stockholders, the bank will seek to have each of you sign for 100 percent of the loan. During negotiations, ask your banker if each of you can sign for 20 percent of the loan, for a total guarantee of 100 percent.

I handled a negotiation like this for a surveying and mapping company in Massachusetts. The company had five major stockholders, and the bank wanted a 100 percent personal guarantee on a $100,000 loan from each stockholder. Technically, the bank could collect $500,000 on a $100,000 loan by having each partner sign. If you and your four partners sign and the loan goes bad, the bank may decide to go after you because you've got the most assets or the deepest pockets. You will then have to sue your partners to have them take responsibility for their share of the loan. That could turn into a long legal mess, and it's not some remote possibility—it happens all the time.

When I went into negotiations for the Massachusetts company, we asked that the personal guarantee be split five ways, so that each stockholder was responsible for $20,000. The bank didn't want to do it because it's much more expensive for the bank to have to sue five people for $20,000 each than it is to sue one person for $100,000. Depending on how the loan guarantee is written, there is often a jury trial, and in most states today it takes about six years just to get a jury trial. Also, the contract statute of limitations is usually six years. You should know the facts about personal loan guarantees before you start negotiations. Ask your lawyer to brief you so that you can negotiate intelligently. State laws vary, and you really need good legal advice (and remember, I'm not a lawyer).

Although we didn't come out of the negotiations with a 20 percent guarantee for each stockholder, we did get 50 percent. That's still quite an improvement over 100 percent. Don't hesitate to negotiate. The bank wants to lend you the money, and you need the money. Both parties ought to be able to find some middle ground on all the issues. In the case of the Massachusetts surveying and mapping company, the bank was happy; it had a $250,000 guarantee. The stockholders would have been happier with only 20 percent liability, but they were pleased to have gotten their guarantees halved.

Another negotiable aspect of the guarantee is when it goes into effect. For example, tell your banker that you don't want to sign the personal guarantee, but if your company is late on more than three consecutive loan payments, the personal guarantee will go into effect. With your banker, arrange a scenario that will trigger when the guarantee will go into effect. In this way, you are not guaranteeing the debt unless certain unlikely events occur. Here are a few conditions:

1) You miss three consecutive loan payments.
2) Working capital falls below a specified amount.
3) Net worth falls below a specified amount.

One more thing: Avoid the entrepreneur's innate tendency to act like a blowfish when it comes to filling out the personal financial statement required by the bank. Do not exaggerate the value of your assets; this tactic will only come back to haunt you. Your best bet is not to inflate your net worth, but to show the truth (or a little less than the truth). Keep in mind that the personal loan guarantee and the personal financial statement act as a directory for the bank's lawyer to find where you keep attachable assets (typically real estate) in case your company defaults on the loan.

Negotiating the Loan Agreement

All of the negotiation points we've just discussed are ways to chip away at the personal loan guarantee, but the principles of give-and-take negotiation involved should also be applied when you negotiate the loan itself. Remember, the game is catch, not go-fetch. The concept of chipping away is useful in both situations. Bankers negotiate with entrepreneurs three times a day, but entrepreneurs negotiate with bankers once every few years.

It's common for bankers to work some fairly troublesome loan provisions into a loan agreement. You may find them unfair or too strict, but don't just complain to your banker about them, chip away at them. There is no such thing as boilerplate; every item in a loan agreement is negotiable, depending on your situation.

The following is a list of troublesome loan provisions:

1) Five days to advise you of infraction; via Federal Express, fifteen days.
2) One week to cure a default, substitute fifteen business days.
3) The word "material" should modify declaration of default. For example, leasing capital equipment prevents renting a photocopier.
4) Inequitable Provisions
   a) Bank mistakes against you to which you fail to call attention within 30 days are forfeited.
   b) Bank mistakes in your favor that you don't catch can be corrected by the bank at any time (no time limit).
5) Exceptions for restrictions, such as working capital, 30-day exception for seasonality, etc.

For example, if the bank wants a notice period of five days to advise you of an infraction of the loan contract, ask your banker for ten business days. That's quite a difference, isn't it? Or, if your loan agreement offers you a grace period of one week to cure a default, ask to substitute fifteen business days to assure that you'll have enough time after written notice of the default is received.

Also watch for a list of petty technical violations that would put the loan into default. Your loan agreement may prevent you from leasing "capital equipment." Does that include an office copier? You may not think so, but technically, it does; and if your loan officer comes under pressure to trim his loan portfolio, he could use this technicality to keep you playing go-fetch. Often the loan officer is overridden by bank regulators, and the letter and the spirit of the "law" can be quite opposite. Make sure the word "material" is used to modify a declaration of default.

Watch for inequitable provisions in the loan agreement, and don't hesitate to challenge your banker on them. If you look carefully, you might find that bank mistakes against you to which you fail to call attention within 30 days are forfeited, while bank mistakes in your favor that you don't catch can be corrected by the bank at any time. Ask your banker to delete or modify such an imbalanced provision. You can also negotiate exceptions for restrictions placed by the loan agreement on your working capital. Let's say the agreement requires you to maintain net working capital of $250,000 at all times, but your business experiences a slump in inventory every April. Ask your banker for a 30-day suspension of the provision during that time.

If you practice these examples of how to use the principle of chipping away on your loan agreement, you'll be an expert negotiator by the time you reach the personal loan guarantee!

One more thing: Don't offer to fill out your bank's preprinted personal financial statement. If you do, you are tacitly agreeing to sign the personal loan guarantee. Let your banker raise the subject. When he does, remind him of the value of the assets already included in your business plan. I suggest not filling in the bank's forms for personal finances. Substitute a signed and notarized form that you have prepared ahead of time, which gives the same level of information.

Talk to your lawyer before filling out the financial statement. You pay your lawyer high fees; use him or her for advice early on because the fees become higher if you get into trouble. Find out from your lawyer how much information you can withhold while staying within the bounds of generally accepted legal procedure. Lawyers, bless their little hearts, are all well versed in handling this delicate subject. If putting down that expensive second home bothers you, maybe it's time to sell it and put the money into your business.

How to Keep off Personal Guarantees in the First Place

If you are new to getting loans for your business and you've never signed a personal loan guarantee, read this section slowly and carefully. The best thing you can do for your future is avoid signing for your loans from the very start. Remember your banker's long elephant-like memory? No banker has ever said to a customer who has been on personal loan guarantees, "Gee, you're such a good customer of the bank, I don't think we need to bother with these silly guarantees any more." No matter how hard you work at becoming your banker's best friend and customer, if you signed personal loan guarantees in the beginning, she'll never forget it. She'll expect you to sign them from now until you die, no matter how successful you become. In practice, most CEOs get off personal loan guarantees by switching banks. The entrepreneur walks into the new bank across the street and says, "I'll bring my business to your bank—same terms and conditions—but no personal guarantees. What do you say?" According to my research, that's how about half of all guarantees are released in the real world.

The first step is the same as that for getting off a personal loan guarantee: Decide what it's worth to you to avoid signing.

Early in the history of your business, ask your board of directors to vote on this resolution: "Officers and shareholders of this corporation will not be allowed to sign personally for any debt. Any debt for which they sign personally will not be honored by this corporation." Have this resolution signed, dated, notarized, and put in your minutes book. Renew it by voting on it at every annual meeting.

When you are asked by your banker to personally guarantee your first loan, you can moan and pull out your minutes book. Show her what a tremendous hassle it's going to be for you to go to the board of directors and change company policy. Bankers love to tell you, "It's our policy." Fight policy with policy.

One of our CEO Club members, Dr. Charles Feldman of Cardio-Data in Sudbury, Massachusetts, heard me give this advice ten years ago. He was buying a large piece of medical equipment for his business, and the supplier wanted him to sign a personal loan guarantee. The delivery man waltzed into Charles's office with the personal guarantee for him to sign. Charles said, "Gee, I never knew when I ordered the CAT scan machine that you were going to require a personal guarantee. That wasn't even discussed."

Of course the delivery man said, "Well, I can't just leave it here. This piece of equipment is worth three times your whole company. You have to be responsible for it."

Charles pulled out his minutes book and showed him nine years of annual corporate minutes to the effect that no officer of the corporation may sign personal guarantees on corporate purchases.

"Do you know what I would have to do to undo this?" Charles said. "I'd have to call a meeting of the stockholders. The stockholders will have to elect new directors. I don't know what they're going to do—this could take nine months! I can't sign that thing. If I do, I could be criminally prosecuted for going against the rules of the board of directors."

Now, bet in court for about five seconds, but it is a useful and often convincing negotiating tool. In Charles's case, it worked on the truck driver. Every little "policy" helps.

After you show your minutes book to your loan officer and moan about company policy, ask her if everyone signs personally for loans at her bank. Even if all you do is ask this question, you're ahead. You're showing that you're no dummy.

Finally, try offering another piece of collateral as a means of staying off a personal loan guarantee. If you have a second home, offer it as collateral; an assignment on your second home is better than a personal blanket guarantee on everything you own. By doing this, you protect your primary homestead.

Don't hesitate to mention Lee Iacocca. Try this approach:

"When Chrysler found itself in trouble and borrowed all that money, Lee Iacocca didn't have to sign a personal guarantee for the money, did he? Did any members of Chrysler's team have to guarantee the debt? Why should I? I'm not borrowing as much money as they did, and my company certainly is not in as bad shape as Chrysler was at that time. The likelihood that Iacocca was going to turn Chrysler around was less than the likelihood that I'm going to keep my profitable business profitable. Why should I have to sign personally for my small loan for my solid company?"

Don't be afraid to get indignant!

"It's not fair! Banks pick on little guys like me and let the big guys like Iacoca off the hook! It's discrimination against the backbone of the U.S. economy—the entrepreneur—and if you don't believe me, just think of the millions of small farmers in the Midwest who are being discriminated against by an unfair double standard!"

Your banker will probably say something like this:

"Well, Chrysler is a public company, and public companies are not controlled by their officers."

Here's a comeback:

"Public company, oh yeah? Tell me, what was Lee Iaccoca's salary for the year he got that debt package. That's right, it was $1.00. And what was his salary the year he saved the business? It was $20.6 million! Public company, baloney! That sure sounds like an entrepreneurial company to me! I tell you, the damn banking system is just plain unfair to the little guy."

From the policy in your company minutes and your "Matilda" story to this tirade against injustice, your banker will get the picture: *You don't take personal guarantees lightly.*

Do not let your nonworking spouse cosign your loan (by nonworking I mean not working with you in the business). It used to be common procedure for a businessman to take his loan agreement home to his wife for her to sign somewhere between cooking dinner and putting the kids to bed. Nowadays, though, more and more women are bringing home loan agreements for their husbands to cosign (male spouses are being asked to autograph the dotted line even more than wives these days). The days of automatic signing of a personal loan guarantee by a spouse are over. Nonetheless, your banker will probably hand the loan agreement to you and say, "Okay, just take it home and have your wife (or husband) sign it and bring it back tomorrow, and we'll give you the money."

Don't do it. Who are you to speak for your spouse? He or she probably has his or her own business to sign for or his or her own assets to protect. Pressuring your spouse to sign the guarantee is the kind of thing that destroys a relationship and causes trouble.

Make it tough for your banker to ask for your spouse's signature. Tell her, "I understand your policy is to have my wife sign. It's just that Mary doesn't really understand the necessity of this. She wants to talk to you herself. I can't really speak for her on this. I'm sorry, but I really have little choice on this one. You're going to have to talk to her yourself about having her sign, and I honestly don't see how this bank can be so chauvinistic as to require my spouse to do this. After all, she is just an innocent, uninformed third party." Let your spouse defend himself or herself. I find this is the best way to keep your spouse off the guarantee. He or she usually makes a pretty strong case for not being part of the personal guarantee. (You can always tell your spouse to say, "Did Lee Iacocca's wife have to sign personally for his loan for Chrysler?") Ask your lawyer about recent court cases concerning the liabilities of innocent spouses; they are increasingly being decided in favor of the spouse.

Build Your Case Piece by Piece

Don't forget to decide how much it is really worth to you to avoid signing personally, so you don't get carried away during the negotiations. Start by telling your banker how much it would mean to your peace of mind not to have to sign. Tell her the "Matilda" story, have her meet Matilda, and then, have Matilda mention Lee Iaccoca's wife. Build your case! If you've done your homework and spent some time befriending your banker, she'll be more likely to respond to your plea.

If you do end up having to sign personally for your first loan, don't be discouraged. In the real world, you are part of the 99 percent of CEOs who do sign. At least you got the loan, and now you can put all the strategies you've learned from this book to work on your banker so that you can get off the guarantee you're already on and avoid signing personally for your next loan.

Set future milestones for getting off. Start chipping away at that guarantee from day one. Find out where and when between 0 percent and 100 percent of repayment your banker will let you off the guarantee. As soon as you take out the guarantee, write a letter to your banker letting her know that the guarantee was not given lightly, and that it bothers you.

Homesteading

One final thing to look into is homesteading your primary residence. In the last century, many states enacted legislation stating that a lender who lent you money for an asset other than your primary residence could not take your principal residence toward payment on a loan. In simple language it meant that if a farmer bought a tractor and he stopped making payments on it, the lender couldn't confiscate the farm. The farmer could file a piece of paper called the Homestead Act to protect his principal residence.

The good news is that in more than half the states, the Homestead Act still exists, and many lawyers recommend that you homestead your home. Depending on the state, you file one sheet of paper with the registrar of deeds in your town, and it protects a certain amount of equity in the home (in some states, homesteading is automatic, and you don't need to file anything). In Massachusetts, for example, it protects $40,000 of the equity in your home. If your home is worth $100,000 and a secondary lender (not the banker who has the mortgage on your home) tries to take your home to pay a debt on which you've defaulted, he has to leave $40,000 of equity in the home. The fact that you've filed the Homestead Act on your home is not common knowledge, either. It might not show up when you fill out the loan application or the personal financial information unless the bank decides to do a title search, which is rarely done unless you are specifically pledging the home as collateral. See your lawyer about whether your home might qualify for homesteading. It offers good protection—another step in the strategy of getting off personal loan guarantees.

The states of Florida, Texas, and Oklahoma have outstanding homestead protection. In these entrepreneurial states, you can protect the entire homestead and all its equity. Always speak to your lawyer, though, to make sure you're up-to-date on any recent changes in state laws.

I never said it would be easy to get off personal loan guarantees, but it is certainly possible if you follow the step-by-step strategy I have given in this book. A good negotiating plan will increase your probability of getting off personal loan guarantees, just as a good business plan guides the growth of your business. In each case, you set goals and work toward achieving those goals.

If you go away with just one thought from this book, I hope it will be that, just like the rest of us, a banker is a human being and, like any human being, she responds to warmth and friendly interest in herself. Do all your research and have all the facts and figures she needs, but don't forget to treat her as you would any friend from whom you want a favor. Be her best customer, and you'll get off those personal loan guarantees. And remember, the best way to get off a personal loan guarantee is not to sign the damn thing in the first place!

The Five C's of Credit

When it comes to loans, bankers are looking for answers to a series of questions that fall under five categories: character, capital, capacity, collateral and guarantees, and conditions. The various ingredients that are included in a thorough request will address these questions.

1) Character. Who are you? How long have you lived where you live? How long have you been in business? Do you live up to your obligations? What is your standing in the community? (The answers to these questions come from your business plan.) What is your credit history? Have you always repaid your obligations? What do your suppliers say about you? What about your personal credit history? How will your credit history reflect on your credit future? (The answers to these questions come from your credit history and references.)

2) Capital. Do you have adequate resources to support your request? Are your assets sound? Does your business have a positive net worth? Do you have sound personal financial statements?

3) Capacity. What is your ability to repay the loan? How are the loan proceeds to be used? How will they be repaid? (The answers to these questions come from a review of your financial statements, particularly your cash flow statements, profit and loss statements, and personal and corporate tax returns.)

4) Collateral and Guarantees. How can you be sure of your ability to repay the loan? What can you offer the bank as an alternative source of repayment? (The answers to these questions come from your projected cash flow statements and your list of assets.) In most instances, the bank will require the personal guarantees of all principals. Besides providing another source of repayment, it also shows your commitment to the business.

5) Conditions. What is the state of the economy? Are there environmental issues to be concerned about? How could these affect the financial condition of your business?

Borrower's Checklist

- Have you prepared your financial data?
- Balance Sheet.
- Profit and Loss Statements for the next three years and for the past three years (if possible).
- Cash Flow Statement.
- Projected Balance Sheet.
- Make copies of tax returns for the past three years.
- Create and include a detailed budget for your business.
- Include a copy of your business plan.
- Obtain written credit reports and references on you and your business.
- Prepare a list of collateral and/or reserves.
- Take out a life insurance policy that will repay your debts in the event of your death.
- Make a list of inventory, tools, equipment, furniture, and other assets.
- Determine the worth of your business based on current market values.
- Collect all deeds, titles, insurance policies, and other legal documents relating to you and your business.

- Prepare your business for an on-site visit from your loan officer.
- Include a detailed marketing plan and provide your loan officer with any promotional materials about your business (brochures, ads, articles, press releases).
- Open an account with the bank you hope to borrow from.
- Organize your data into a cohesive and attractive written loan request. Don't forget to include a cover letter.
- Develop a relationship with your banker.

Tips for Preparing Documents

1) Be sure your statements are neat and legible.
2) Statements should be prepared by your accountant; always review figures for any errors or omissions.
3) Date your statements to coincide with the date of your figures.
4) Keep projections, assets lists, and collateral statements on the conservative side.
5) Update financial information annually and forward copies to your banker.
6) Remember, your banker cannot make a decision until all of your documentation has been received. To ensure a speedy response, make sure your application is complete.

Chapter 4

Buying a Business

How to Screen the Deal Flow

How do you efficiently, effectively decide which of the thousands of deals now coming across your desk each month are worthy of further investigation?

The Venture Time-ist

First you must develop an information checklist to see whether this deal meets your basic needs. Just like the venture capitalist who, after five minutes perusing a business plan, can decide whether to meet the principals or toss the proposal in the trash bin, you must be able to quickly size up a proposed deal. You, after all, are a venture time-ist.

The venture capitalist is someone who manages a fund of money, usually acquired from a group of investors, by placing it in appropriate business enterprises. Venture capitalists target an overall annual return on their money of 40 or 50 percent or more. However, in practice, they are lucky to realize half that lofty objective. If they did not shoot for 45 percent, they surely would not be able to obtain a rate of return necessary to justify the risk.

Venture time-ists, on the other hand, do not have capital to invest, or if they do, they do not choose to invest the capital in new enterprises. Instead, the venture time-ist seeks to invest time, ideas, savvy, and brain work in an enterprise in order to obtain a return in the form of cash.

Be wary of becoming a venture out-of-time-ist. Careful thought and good ideas should stretch your time and make your search more effective, despite the number of deals facing you. Use your own brain power and experience to develop your own checklists. Custom design your checklists into a set of ever-finer sieves through which to run your deal flow. Initial sieves will relate to the broad questions of whether or not your needs are met. Later sieves narrow the flow by examining the specific deal in depth for potential sales levels, hidden opportunities or problems, legal and financial details, and similar due diligence factors. Your screening is a process of constantly narrowing your field, not a one-time event.

Now let's construct the first level or two of sieves. Remember, there is more art to the process than science. One person's good deal can be another person's problem.

What do you really need to know up front? First, you want to know if the business meets your own criteria. Second, you need to know whether the business can be financed, given your situation. Third, you need to know whether the business is a "good" deal.

Does It Meet Your Criteria?

Is it really in your targeted industry, or does it take your team outside its expertise? If every manager quit when you took over, how comfortable would you be running the show? How long would it be before you were at 95 percent efficiency? Note we're looking for visceral responses, not numbers; you want to quickly screen the likely deals from the unlikely.

Include criteria about the number of employees and number of managers who will stay with the new buyer. This information can help you determine if the business is going to be manageable by your team.

Where is the business located? Is there a long-term lease? Why is the business located where it is? Most businesses are movable, many at a low cost. Don't initially get hung up on the idea that a business might not be located where you would want to live. Then again, a favorable long-term lease might more than outweigh the savings from moving the business closer to its suppliers or customers. What are the weaknesses in the management team? There is no such thing as a business without weaknesses. If the owner will not admit to any weaknesses, he or she might be unrealistic in other aspects of the negotiations, too. What you are really looking for is to see if the weaknesses in the business match the strengths on your team.

Is the profit level high enough to pay your team's salaries and give a good return on investment? Remember that your salaries are not part of your return on investment, unless you like working for nothing. Many buyers miss this point because of its simplicity. Buying a business is an expensive alternative to securing a job.

Is it a good deal even if it isn't profitable? First, many business failures are caused by "pilot error." Second, doing a turnaround in a business you know might be easier than taking over a profitable business where the owner's personality dominated the business and the customers are likely to disappear when the owner leaves. Finally, a losing business that has a patent you could use, a distribution system in place that complements yours, a key piece of property that fits your needs, or a product line that can fill holes in your own product line might be worth buying because of your particular needs. In business, two plus two can equal five. Check for synergy.

Can It Be Financed?

You'll need to determine if the business can be financed readily or whether an inordinate amount of effort and persuasion will be required. It is often easier to finance a business with a tangible product, as opposed to a service business. A product-oriented business has accounts receivable, inventory, and fixed assets, much of which can serve as collateral for a bank or other type of loan. A service business typically has little in the way of bankable assets. If you are buying a $10 million manufacturing facility that has $5 million worth of equipment and $5 million worth of inventory, you will find it easier to finance than if you were buying a service business with $6,000 worth of office equipment for $100,000. For this reason, obtain a current balance sheet early. The seller will often initially send just the income statement, because he thinks you are only interested in current income. Insist on seeing the balance sheet because you are buying a package that includes financing, and the balance sheet quickly gives you the most useful information about the business. By the time you are ready to buy, you must see all the financial statements; but as a first quick cut, get the balance sheet.

But are service businesses wholly unfinancable? If you reject all service businesses, you will have rejected 60 percent of all businesses in the United States today. That percentage will continue to grow. Aren't we all really in the service business? Take a look at IBM, one of the largest manufacturing companies in the world today. What have they traditionally advertised? Not their machines, but their people and what those people provide: service. So be careful not to prematurely sort out all service businesses, especially if your experience is in service businesses. Owners of service businesses know they aren't bankable, so they are often willing to take a few extra steps to provide the financing themselves.

There are several ways to finance a service business. For example, professional practices, such as accounting practices, are typically sold on a multiple of client billings. The price is often paid as a percentage of gross revenues actually received over two, three, or four years after the sale. The price might be, say, 45 percent of all receipts of the first year, 35 percent of the second year, 25 percent of the third year, and 15 percent of the fourth year.

Therefore, if you are evaluating a service business, you should gauge the owner's willingness and ability to provide the financing. For instance, you might ask the seller, "How much cash do you need to have at closing?" Or you might ask what the seller plans to do with the sale proceeds. If the money needs to be used for pressing medical bills, you have a poor candidate to provide financing. You might politely inquire what levels of payment the seller would be likely to need and for how long.

Whether the business is service- or product-oriented, you will want to determine if the income is subject to seasonal fluctuations. Since making level monthly payments is easier if you have level monthly income, the business without great monthly fluctuations will be easier to finance.

Is real estate included? Most people are pretty sophisticated when valuing real estate, so you seldom obtain a bargain price. If the seller is willing to separate the building from the business, and lease it to you with an option to buy, that can provide a big chunk of your financing. On the other hand, if there are not many tangible assets in the business, a piece of real estate might make your deal "bankable." Or you might be able to sell the building at a gain and move into less expensive quarters, using the cash from the sale to cut down your debt burden.

Although it need not be a line on your checklist, be on the lookout for a business that is in or near bankruptcy. The business has creditors already in place. If you can increase their chances of getting more than 10 cents on the dollar, you just might be able to take over financing which is already in place. Bankrupt companies can be good businesses. The bankruptcy might have been caused by "pilot error," and you might be a better "pilot." As a rule of thumb, with exceptions, many of the best leveraged buyouts (LBOs) are generated out of bankruptcy. Robert McCray, now an "angel" in New Hampshire, bought Worcester Control out of bankruptcy. He was a salesman who converted a lot of brains and a little money into a business he sold for millions of dollars years later.

Is It a Good Deal?

You want to get a workable overall view of the deal as quickly as possible, which involves not only running the numbers but doing an internal interest level check on yourself and your team members. If after the initial review you can't get excited about the deal, you probably won't be able to later, and it's your enthusiasm and excitement for a deal that will sell your financing package, as well as make a go of the business in the long run.

You are not just looking for the seller's answers to questions, but for the reactions of the seller as well. Buyer and seller must develop a good rapport and trust. Some face-to-face contact is therefore essential and usually saves time if undertaken early in the process.

Here are the questions that should be on your checklist:

1) **How long has the business been for sale?** The first few deals you uncover will be the ones on the market the longest. If it has

been an inordinate length of time, say, more than six months to one year, there is probably something wrong with the deal. Most often, it is an unrealistic attitude on the part of the seller toward price or toward providing financing. This problem is not necessarily a go/no-go factor (very few of the questions you ask are), but it is something for you to weigh in the total balance.

2) **What is your lowest all-cash price?** The answer will give you an idea of whether the business is within your price and financing range. It will also serve to give you a psychological bargaining tool later, because the seller has already openly committed herself to a certain price range.

3) **Why are you selling the business?** Sometimes the advertised reason is the real reason, but often it is not. At the preliminary stage, you are really not in a position to explore the real reasons, so just listen and see if you catch anything between the lines.

4) **What were last month's sales? Profits?** What were the same figures for last quarter? For last year? From this information, you can determine if the business is profitable, but you can also discover the owner's astuteness. The information can be useful in later bargaining. It also gives you a brief trend to see if the business is going uphill or downhill. A critical supplier could have gone out of business, a large customer could have fallen on hard times or pulled a major order, or a product quality problem could have developed. Nothing ever stays level in life or in business.

5) **Are there any IRS problems?** Are there any other tax problems? This question is, in all likelihood, a surprise for the seller. The answer is one he or she didn't want to let out this early in the game. The most typical IRS problem is not having paid withholding taxes. Not having paid sales taxes runs a close second. It is so easy to keep that money in the till and operate on it that a lot of businesses get stuck; but once the tax man cometh, the situation becomes dire quicly. The seller has to do something now or face an IRS agent who wants to padlock his doors. This situation puts you in a good bargaining position because you can become the potential white knight with the cash to relieve the pressure. Here you need legal advice. It is often possible to get a good deal from the seller, but an even better one directly from the IRS or state tax collector. Payroll taxes are not relieved by Chapter 11 filings; they are then the owner's personal liability.

6) If you're examining businesses in bankruptcy, does the business have a relatively high proportion of noncritical unsecured lenders? A secured lender will usually get its money because of the liens it holds. A critical supplier, one who supplies a product that cannot be duplicated elsewhere without inordinate cost, is in a commanding position to stay on as a supplier if the business continues. The noncritical unsecured lender is at risk to lose the entire amount, or at least 90 cents on the dollar, of everything that is owed. This person is someone with whom you can negotiate; you may be able to work out a deal by which the supplier gives up his claim. You agree to purchase all of your needs from that supplier for the next three years at 2 percent above market, or maybe you can discount his debt by 50 percent or 75 percent. Examples would be printers, filling stations, restaurants, office supply stores, T.V. or radio stations, newspapers, or any other business where there is much competition for your orders.

7) Is the business a corporation, a partnership, or a proprietorship? If it's a corporation, is it an S corporation? The answers will help you determine the tax impact of your proposed purchase and will help you structure it. You will also learn a little bit about the degree of sophistication of the seller.

8) What differentiates you from your competitors? Why is your product or service any better than theirs? This question gives the seller the chance to give you a sales pitch, but it is something you need to know for your own financing efforts, as well as to see whether the company is operated in a way that agrees with your business philosophy. For instance, if you are oriented toward high-quality products or services, and the answer comes out, "We provide the best price in town," you may not want to get involved with this particular deal.

9) Who are your three most direct competitors? The answer gives you people you will visit before you buy (you certainly won't be able to visit them after you buy). It also helps answer the following related question.

10) What business are you in? This question helps you determine if the business owner has thought about the business and has a plan for its future. If you get an elementary answer, you may be more able than present management to grow the business. On the other hand, if you get a sophisticated answer and the business is losing money, chances are slight that you can do any better. If it is both a sophisticated response and a profitable business, you may have a winner.

11) **Who do you owe the most money?** Is it personally guaranteed? The answers to these questions help you to determine the financability of the deal. If there is a large amount of personally guaranteed money outstanding, it might be difficult to merely assume that debt, because the seller often wants to be released when you close your purchase. If the seller does agree to remain liable, you might find it easier to assume that financing, because the lender has two sources of repayment securing the debt. If the money is not personally guaranteed, it indicates a degree of confidence by the creditors in the ability of the business alone to service the debt. (*See Chapter 3, Bank Loans*)

12) **What makes this business a good opportunity for me?** Again you are giving the seller a chance to make a sales pitch. If you haven't heard any good news by this point, you might as well walk away.

13) **If I invested $100,000 in your business today, but required that it not be used to pay outstanding debts, how would you spend it?** The answer gives you an insight into the seller's dreams for the business and where it might be able to go. Good insider ideas on improving the business are invaluable. You will have plenty of your own, but the wisdom that comes from experience should always be sought.

14) **What do you plan to do with the money you receive?** How is your personal tax situation going to affect what you do with the money? The information here is personal, so it is often difficult to get in any great detail. Try a little finesse. The information is necessary to enable you to generate creative solutions to the problem of financing and sometimes even to the question of the price. Even if you get it in bits and pieces, it's worth being persistent.

15) **What percentage of the purchase price must be cash at closing?** The answer is another clue to financing from the owner. Be careful to ask the question this way so you don't lock in the seller. If she says, "Read my lips—no financing" this early, you could have a tough time getting her to change her position later. Financing from an owner generally is easier to get the closer you get to closing.

So the best bet is to be low-key and play a little dumb on this issue. Remember, you're still selling.

Business Investigation Checklist

You have focused on one or two businesses that look promising. How do you perform your investigation?

There are no perfect deals out there. What you should seek is the deal which reduces your risk to a reasonable level, one in which you have most (but likely not all) of your requirements and desires met. To paraphrase Henry Ford, "To be successful, all I have to do is be right 51 percent of the time, and make many decisions." Carry that attitude into your search, and you may do as well as Henry Ford!

You will not want to do every one of the following things to investigate every deal, and for some deals you will want to do more. Don't follow any checklist blindly. Adjust each checkpoint to meet your particular needs.

Financial Checklist

1) Make sure your attorney and accountant both check out the financials. They'll provide insights and points of view you couldn't figure on your own.
2) Has management or the owner prepared financial projections? If so, get as many as you can.
3) What bank or banks does the business work with? What services do they get from each bank? Contact these banks.
4) Are there any appraisals of the business or any of its assets made within the last five or ten years? If so, get copies.
5) Get an aging of accounts receivable, both current and at the end of each of the last three years.
6) Get a list of the principal suppliers of the business, including how long each one has been a supplier and who the alternate suppliers are. What are the terms of sale for each? Are there any long-term purchase commitments?

7) Visit the suppliers of the business. Try to talk to the particular salespeople who call on this account. Ask them what they know about the business and whether it is worth buying. These people know how well the business is doing compared to similar businesses.

8) Check with noncompeting businesses in the area (such as the business owner next door) to see how well your target is doing.

9) Check with local business associations to find out how your target business is doing. The local Better Business Bureau is also a good stop to find out if there are many complaints against the business.

10) Check with former owners and with competitors about how well the business is doing. They might not tell you everything you need to know, but it wouldn't hurt to have a few extra clues.

11) Check with similar businesses in noncompeting geographic areas. They might also be able to tell you what to look for in this particular business, and they might also be interested in selling if your deal falls through.

12) Sit down without the benefit of actual financial statements in front of you and see if you can list what items you would expect to affect the sales in this type of business. Then list what should go into making up the cost of sales. List what expenses would probably be needed to run the business and the necessary equipment. Then take your lists and look at the financials. Are there missing items or any additions? If so, you have new questions to ask.

13) If the postage meter is fat, the company is fat; if it's skinny, the company is skinny. Look particularly at the beginning of a month or the beginning of a year to see how much postage is in the machine. (It's easy to do—if you don't know how, the secretary or mail clerk who runs the machine can show you.) Some businesses have been known to use the postage meter to get a big tax deduction for postage at the end of the year, and then take the postage meter back to the post office for a refund early in the following year. It is also an easy place to save or even hide excess cash.

14) The backs of checks provide many little (and not so little) pieces of information about the business. You may find that certain checks to employees are always cashed at the Country Saloon or that business expense reimbursement checks made out to the owner are consistently cashed at a resort 500 miles away.

15) It is getting harder for purchasers to buy the tax loss carryforwards of the prior owner; but if they can be purchased, it can make a good deal even better. Don't go shopping for tax loss carryforwards, but be alert to their possible existence.

16) Look particularly for checking account deposits in round numbers. Customer payments are hardly ever in round dollars. Are they loans to the business? Are they transfers in and out? What is going on with these "odd" deposits?

17) Make sure you get the bylaws and minute books. Don't just hand them to your lawyer—you'll get more out of them than she will. If there is anything unusual or significant going on, you will see it here. The bylaws are generally pretty standard, so get a set from your lawyer or the local library so you can isolate unusual provisions. Then start with the most recent minutes and work your way backward for three to five years until you feel comfortable with what you're finding. You will see things such as authorizations of bonus or retirement plans, grants of stock options (who will you have to buy out?), awards of fringe benefits, leases of property to or from "insiders," and licensing, royalty, or franchise agreements. A quick skim is really all that is necessary to review internal and external audit reports and management recommendation letters.

18) Review internal and external audit reports and management recommendation letters.

19) Review tax audit reports and determine if there are any extensions of time to complete audits or any audits still in process.

20) Review reports filed with any and all state and federal agencies.

History of the Business

1) When was the business founded? What was its original name, and what other names has it had?

2) What was the company's original line of business, and how did it get started with its current product line?

3) What are the names of all of its subsidiaries and divisions? When did each start business, and what is the function of each?

Marketing and Competition

1) What is the company's main business? Be careful. This is a trick question. The business may be different from what management thinks it is. For instance, railroad companies that defined themselves as railroads in the early 1900s lost business to trucking companies. Those that redefined themselves as transportation companies saw the possibility of additional markets, went after them, and kept their businesses alive and vital.

Ask this question not only of the management and current owners, but also of yourself. If you are looking at a hardware store, is its business to supply hardware items, or is it to provide information and supplies to people to improve their homes? The difference is more than semantics. It might be the difference between survival and failure.

2) Get copies of the sales literature and brochures of the company. What kind of an image do they portray?

3) What is the growth potential in this industry? Ask the seller's management, but also ask your own management team. If you don't know, then get someone on your management team to find out. Does the potential that you see match what the seller sees? What is the reason for the difference?

4) Who are the competitors? This may also be a trick question. For instance, if you are looking at a local office supply store, the competitors may not be the other office supply stores in town. The major competition might be the mail order house from the big city 300 miles away.

Your seller may not have focused on this issue. If not, don't alert her.

5) How do the company's products or services differ from the competition's? What makes the products or services any better? What niche is the company aiming to serve?

6) What are the sales trends and patterns for each product or service? Is demand seasonal? Are the trends and patterns cyclical over a period of years? For instance, are the sales up for three years at a stretch and then down for one or two?

7) Is the market dominated by large companies or many small ones? If it's controlled by a large company, you might find yourself trying to fight a giant that can underprice you and sit back waiting for you to fold. On the other hand, a fragmented market might mean that there are no real leaders, and the business could be out the door the minute somebody undercuts your price by one-tenth of one percent.

8) How closely tied are the sales to the personality of the owner or key managers? If that person leaves, will the business leave with him or her? This situation is difficult to assess. A survey of customers or potential customers might provide clues.

A true story can help us see how serious this issue is, and how tough it is to spot. Ziggie P. owned a large auto repair shop. This shop usually had ten to fifteen mechanics and was extremely busy. It had a lot of innovative practices, such as staying open evenings. Ziggie was getting the mortgages paid off and even finding time away from the business to go fishing.

But then Ziggie became extremely ill. There was a time when it wasn't known whether or not he would live. He was away from the shop for almost ten months. Although the shop ran well when he was away, when word of his serious condition got out, business began drifting away. Ziggie's wife and management did much to keep the business going. They had sales. They ran ads in the paper. They contacted the usual referral sources. Nothing reversed the trend.

Then, just when it looked like the doors would have to close on Ziggie's shop, Ziggie started getting well. Almost as soon as Ziggie started coming back to the shop half-days twice a week, the business picked up. Ziggie's shop is now doing well, and Ziggie is back to almost full-time, but his case is instructive. In most small businesses, even when it does not appear to be the case, sales levels can be tied to the owner more than you suspect. It pays to be extremely sensitive to this fact, because if you buy from a Ziggie and your Ziggie flies to Florida with the cash the day after closing, your business may disappear almost as quickly as the jet stream from Ziggie's plane.

9) Check statistical information about the market from sources such as the Wall Street Journal, trade associations, and government reports. Contact the Small Business Administration for government reports. The public library has surprisingly detailed information if you get some help from a reference librarian.

10) There is a magazine or newsletter for just about every occupation and business imaginable. Some get extremely specific when it comes to the group of people they serve. If you have a university library nearby, it would pay to visit the periodical section. If you can't find an actual copy of the magazine or newsletter, find out some likely candidates. Write the periodicals in question and ask for subscription information and sample copies.

11) Visit your local library and get a copy of the last two census reports. Page through and ask yourself questions about what you see in those reports and how they might affect this business. Is the population of your target county increasing or decreasing? Is the population becoming more blue collar or more white collar? Is the income increasing or decreasing? Will this help or hurt your business? There are interim census reports available to update your research—don't rely on stale information...

12) Visit your local telephone company and newspaper advertising departments. Ask them for rate information for advertisers and for market data. You will find a wealth of information that these sources have spent a great deal of money and effort gathering. Some of it will be information that is not available through the local Chamber of Commerce, another good place to check.

13) Of course, there is the Internet which has more information on it than any one person can use!

Marketing and Product Development

1) Does the company sell through its own salespeople or through manufacturer's representatives? If through its own salespeople, are they compensated by commission, by salary, or both? What is the precise compensation structure? Just what does such a structure promote? Get copies of all contracts, peruse them yourself, and have your attorney review them.

2) Are the products distributed locally or nationwide?

3) Who are the principal customers? You might not be able to get the names until you get close to closing, but you might be able to get descriptions of the types of companies. Are the customers in an expanding or declining industry? How well do they pay? How well do the top five customers pay? Are any of the top ten customers in financial trouble? Are any old-time customers starting to pay more slowly than in the past?

4) Try to get the sales volume for the top ten customers for the last three years. Trace whether or not a particular customer is moving away from the company or increasing its dependence. Is your target too dependent on one or two key customers?

5) Have any larger customers been lost? This question is different from the prior one, because a seller could just give you a list of only the current large customers.

6) Do the sales usually involve maintenance agreements, or expressed or implied warranties? Has the company experienced any product liability claims? What are the rates of warranty and maintenance claims?

7) Have there been any new products introduced in the market that make the company's products less competitive or even obsolete? Have any new competitors entered the market?

8) Is the company involved in any research and development? Have the expenditures for R&D tended to grow or diminish over the last few years? What does the

company expect to spend in the next few years? The answers can give clues to future sales potential.

9) What has been the bad debt experience of the company? Ask for a listing of sales and shipment dates by each of the major customers, along with the dates of payments of those invoices for the last year or two. This listing might point out some slow-paying customers. How does the volume of slow-paying accounts affect your cash flow projections?

10) Is the product potentially dangerous to the end-user? One of the big problems these days is what happens if your product explodes or injures somebody in some way. Who is liable for it? If you buy the company, are you picking up liability for products that were improperly manufactured or designed in the past? This field is a quickly developing area of the law, and there are no black-and-white answers. The trend is to have product liability go with the holder of the assets. In other words, even if you buy assets (not stock) of the corporation, you could be held liable for improperly manufactured products, even though you were not the one who manufactured them. Two things you need to do are consult with your attorney about your exposure and what can be done to limit it, and consult with your product liability insurance carrier to see what coverages are available (if any). Make sure you get coverage for past acts.

11) Does the company have a proprietary product, or is it a job shop? If you are manufacturing to specification, then you are essentially a service business. The personality of the owner in that situation could be a key element in the success of your target.

12) Review present and planned advertising campaigns. What are the costs and terms of the contracts, if any? What would you be bound to do? Review sales brochures for quality and effectiveness, but also for overpromising, which can lead to lawsuits. It might not be a bad idea to have legal counsel look at them, too.

13) Would you buy this product or service at this price? This question is always a good litmus test.

Assets

1) Get a complete depreciation schedule for all assets of the business. This schedule will tell you how old the equipment is, and will give you clues as to whether there will be any recapture taxes that may have to be paid by the seller. This information can help you to structure the tax treatment of the deal. Also ask for a list of all equipment currently on order.

2) Are there any leased facilities? If so, get a listing and copies of all of the leases. Actually read the leases. Sure, they're long and boring, but if you read them and the seller goes from memory, you could know something the seller doesn't. This advice is particularly important for leased real estate, since the building and its lease may be essential to the continuation of the business. In many businesses, location is the main element of success.

For example, Gary H. used the lease as a backup to his negotiations to buy a small retail shop. There were no competitors in the vicinity, and no competitors could move in because all of the other likely storefronts were occupied by thriving businesses. Gary found the landlord and negotiated a lease to begin in a few months when the business owner's lease expired. Was this ethical? You decide for yourself.

Also look for rights to sublease or assign the lease if you expect to use the property.

3) Check the physical condition of the land and buildings, even if they are only leased. Many leases require the tenant to make all repairs to the building. Even if the lease does not, you need to know whether the landlord is cooperative in this regard. An uncooperative landlord can mean having to pay for repairs yourself and hoping to get the expenses back later. Therefore, it makes sense to check the roof, parking, ceiling (to look for signs of leaks), heating, plumbing, equipment, and similar items to see what shape they are in. You don't need to be an expert; just keep your eyes open and ask questions.

4) Check out the premises and the inventory. Is the inventory covered with dust? Is it shop-worn? As the

eminent philosopher Yogi Berra said, "There are a lot of things you can observe just by looking."

5) If you are buying real estate, get title insurance commitments and have your attorney review them.

6) Are there any patents, trademarks, or service marks on which the company relies? If so, have them checked out by patent counsel.

7) Are there trade secret or other nondisclosure agreements? Review them yourself and have your attorney do so as well.

8) Leasehold improvements are often written off when they are purchased or over a short period of time. Sometimes they are not recorded anywhere. There may be some real value hidden in leased premises. If so, and if the asset is removable when your lease terminates, you might have another asset available for financing.

Relationships with Outsiders

1) Are there any licenses required to make the product, occupy the premises, or otherwise open the doors for business? Are all licenses valid, up-to-date, and without outstanding violations?

2) What is the company's safety record? Does it have any Occupational Safety and Health Administration (OSHA) or environmental problems? Most businesses are subject to environmental controls if the business produces anything, has by-products, or dumps anything into the water or the air. It pays to take a tour of the facility, including the back end of the lot, to see if any on-site dumping is going on, and that all environmental regulations are being met. If there are any underground storage tanks, there is a potential for huge liability problems. The same is true if there were ever any underground storage tanks on the premises. According to the environmental laws, if you own the real estate where toxic waste has been dumped, even if you are not the one who dumped it and even if the waste was dumped thirty years before you bought the place, you can be responsible for the entire costs of cleanup. There is no

limit on your liability in environmental cases, so you need to be very sensitive to this problem.

In fact, if your target has dumped toxic wastes at an approved toxic waste disposal site and the company running the disposal site is not handling the waste properly, you can be responsible for the full costs of cleanup, not just your share. You can be held responsible even if you did not buy the stock of the business. Bankers and other lenders are increasingly aware of these issues and are taking a very close look at them.

Be sure to review OSHA and Environmental Protection Agency (EPA) inspection reports and company filings.

3) Are the raw materials readily available? Are prices for supplies stable or volatile?

4) How stable are the relationships between the company and its suppliers? How long has your target been dealing with each of its major suppliers? If for too short a time, you could face defections as a new owner. If for too long a time, the prices being paid could have grown to be noncompetitive.

5) Have your legal counsel check for lawsuits, administrative, or disciplinary actions and review in-house litigation logs.

6) Check for contracts with outsiders such as the government, suppliers, customers, insurance companies, and independent contractors. Get copies of these agreements, peruse them yourself, and have your legal people check them out. All insurance policies should be reviewed by your own insurance advisors.

Locality

1) Visit your local traffic department and see what traffic counts there are for the area of your business. These counts are particularly important for a consumer business.

2) Visit the planning department of your municipality and county and determine what changes are in the works.

If that new highway is to be rerouted away from your location, will the change be good or bad?

3) Check for restrictions, liens, zoning, and licenses that might be necessary. Most of these things can be checked out with local municipal offices, starting with the clerk's office. When it comes to licenses, it makes sense to call the municipal attorney's office and find out what licenses are needed for your type of business. Speak to a deputy attorney, not the receptionist. It could be that your target has been operating without proper licenses, and when it changes hands, the city will want to make sure you have them.

Employees

1) For each officer, director, key employee, and key independent contractor, find out:
   a) Length of service
   b) Business background (get a copy of his or her resume if possible)
   c) Compensation and fringe benefits
   d) Age

2) Does management devote all its time to this business or only 80 percent or 50 percent?

3) Do the key people plan to stay with the business? What can we do to help them want to stay (assuming that's what we want)?

4) Are there any employment contracts? Independent contractor arrangements? If so, get a copy of each of them.

5) Are there any noncompetition agreements or confidentiality agreements between management and the company? Between other people and the company? If so, get a copy of each one. Remember, when you're dealing with management, there is no such thing as a standard form. Many will have additions and cross-outs.

6) Get the organization chart for the business. If one is not already made up, try to get one or make one up with the help of current management.

7) Review actual management functions as well as job descriptions. Check out the personnel files of all the key people.

8) Review employee handbooks, vacation plans, bonus plans, severance plans, and early retirement plans. Do you want to be bound by all the terms?

9) Review claim and insurance files for workmen's compensation and unemployment. Are there many disputes?

10) Have a qualified employee benefits attorney review all health, accident, disability, deferred compensation, life insurance, pension, and profit sharing plans. This person should not be your regular business attorney: You need a specialist. Are you going to be bound to continue these plans? At what cost? Are the plans in full compliance? What will be the cost to bring them up to par?

11) How many employees are there? Get a complete census showing departments, ages, hire dates, and wages.

12) Is there a union? If not, have there been any moves to unionize? When? What were the results?

13) What is the historical labor turnover rate?

14) Try to keep your eyes and ears open for evidences of employee morale when you are touring the place of business. Ask questions of personnel along the way. Listen between the lines.

15) Are there any retirement plans, insurance plans, company cars, or other fringe benefits? If so, get a list of them and of who takes part in each plan.

Ownership

1) List the owners of all outstanding stock, along with their relationships to each other (family, business partner, etc.).

2) Does anybody have a right to acquire stock under stock options or warrants? If so, get copies of these agreements.

3) Are there any buy-sell agreements? Are there any restrictions on the ability to buy or sell the stock, or on its use as collateral?

4) Are there any agreements with banks or other lenders limiting transfers of stock?

5) Are all shares fully paid?

6) Are there any agreements among shareholders, written or oral?

7) Does the person with whom you are dealing control at least 51 percent of the company, even if all options and warrants are exercised? If not, who else must consent before you know you have a binding deal?

8) Has the principal owner's stock been placed in trust or given away?

Personal Tax Returns

1) Take a look at those personal income tax returns. Look in detail at the interest received and paid. If the corporation is involved, the corporation's name or address will appear on the return in several places.

2) Look for personal tax situations that might help you to put together a good package offer that has a better than average chance of being accepted.

3) Look for rents, dividends, leases, credits, and other entries that signify money going between owner and business.

How Do You Get the Personal Income Tax Returns?

More often than not you will hear objections from the seller to this "invasion of my privacy." You need to assure the seller that you are not really interested in any great detail in what her personal financial situation might be, but you are interested in making sure that you see all of the transactions that are going on and have a complete picture of how they might affect your own tax situation before you go ahead with the deal. This point is critical. If the seller has something to hide from you, the odds are strong that it is not visible in the financial statements, and you won't find it until after you own the business— and the problem.

A good way to answer the objection is to say, "I just want to satisfy myself there are no big problems. I don't intend to make any copies. Would it be all right if I just came over to your place or had my accountant go to your accountant's and look at the return without taking any copies?" More often than not, this request works. If not, I suggest you seriously consider walking away. After all, you need to trust the person who makes key representations to you—and the personal tax return can be a big one.

Becoming a Franchisee: Are You Qualified?

The immediate, prideful answer is likely to be, "Yes! I'm qualified to become anything I want to be!" That's a good, positive attitude, but while I am not doubting you or your abilities, I have to issue this caveat: Being a franchisee is not necessarily for everyone. It is neither similar to owning a nonfranchised business, nor is it the same as working for someone else. Being a franchisee is a unique hybrid of both boss and employee—you own and run your franchised outlet, but you follow the system and dictates of the franchisor who has (presumably, anyway) perfected the business. In return for the expertise, support, and established reputation you receive from the franchisor, you pay a percentage of your sales. In the best cases, this is a classic synergistic, win-win situation.

To maintain the middle balance necessary to achieve success in this field, it takes a certain type of personality with very specific working traits and temperaments. What you probably are asking now is: What are these traits and do I have them?

Test Your Franchisee Aptitude

I remember that Donald Boroian, CEO of Francorp, a leading franchise consulting firm, used to say that during franchising's early days, before regulation helped clean up the acts of dubious franchisors, there were two basic and critical criteria for potential franchisees: the check test and the mirror test. First, did the franchisee's check clear the bank? Second, if you held a mirror under his nose, did it fog up, meaning the candidate was still breathing? Furthermore, Donald joked, "…some franchisors did not believe that the mirror test was so important, just as long as the check cleared!"

Of course, this story exemplifies how much times have changed. Even if franchisee screening was not that loose and cynical back then, it sure has come a long way since. In fact, in the marketing and sales survey that I will cite extensively throughout this chapter (explained and described below), nearly 90 percent of the franchisor respondents reported having rejected *financially qualified* franchisee applicants because of lack of other qualifications, which were judged to be more important to the long-term well-being of the franchise.

A properly run franchisor never accepts a franchisee merely because he or she can come up with the money. A franchise that eventually fails due to the choice of an unqualified franchisee costs the franchisor far more in time, money, and reputation than the quick, "easy" infusion of up-front money is ever worth. The days of the "check test" may not be completely gone; there will always be unscrupulous operators—which is why it is important to thoroughly research franchisors—but times have changed!

Today, franchisors obviously know what they want when it comes to franchisees, as demonstrated by the strong, very decisive responses to the aforementioned franchisor survey. To help determine who does (or does not) have these traits, a growing number of franchisors, as indicated by the survey results, have turned to some form of franchisee testing. *How exactly do you measure up against the general traits that these franchisors are looking for?*

To help answer this question, I have gathered some solid data. Donald's company, Francorp, in association with DePaul University, has conducted extensive surveys of franchisors, gathering information from these sources on a number of topics regarding the marketing and sales of franchises. A special section of the most recent edition of this poll asked the franchisors to choose, from a list of two dozen, the traits they found to have been most important among their most successful franchisees. A total of 265 franchisors representing more than 40,000 franchised units responded to this survey.

Are You Suited to Become a Successful Franchisee?

The following test for potential franchisees was prepared with Dr. Harry E. "Bud" Gunn, Ph.D., a clinical psychologist. In addition to writing books and speaking on a variety of psychology-related topics, Dr. Gunn specializes in developing tests to assist various industries and corporations in hiring and evaluating personnel.

Starting with the raw data from the Francorp/DePaul franchisors survey, this diagnostic test was created based on its responses. In order to determine your potential for success as a franchisee, answer each question to the best of your ability. The test will be most useful if you answer each question as accurately as you can in terms of your own feelings and experiences, rather than providing the answer that you think a candidate should provide to be a successful franchisee.

Remember, this test is designed to measure your aptitude to be a franchisee, not your worth as a person or your overall general business acumen. As I have noted, the life and career of a franchisee is not for everyone, and it is important to find out if it is right for you before investing considerable time and money to explore specific options within franchising.

Before you take this test, you may wish to obtain a copy of a similar profile, "Do You Have What It Takes to Be an Entrepreneur?" which I developed several decades ago through the Center for Entrepreneurial Management (CEM). This 26-question "Entrepreneur's Quiz" has been very popular and has appeared in *Playboy*, *Penthouse*, and a host of other publications. It was developed in a similar manner to this franchise test from data gathered from approximately 3,000 dues-paying members of CEM. The profiles of the two types of franchisees and entrepreneurs are, as you may imagine, quite different. For a copy, send $10.00 to: Dr. Joe Mancuso, The Center for Entrepreneurial Management, Inc., 180 Varick Street, Penthouse, New York, NY 10014, tel. (212) 633-0060, facsimile (212) 633-0063.

The *Only* Franchise Test You Need to Take

For questions 1-16, please circle the answer that *best* describes you or that you *most agree* with (depending on what the question asks).

1) I have generally been regarded as:
- a) one who loves to plan vacations.
- b) always being willing to work hard.
- c) one who seeks benefits and rewards for my work.
- d) being easy to supervise.

2) Financially, I:
- a) am very conservative.
- b) am very liberal.
- c) have always been able to put money aside.
- d) have never been well off.

3) Taking directions from others is:
- a) one of my strong talents.
- b) something I do not like.
- c) often a must.
- d) acceptable if not constantly required.

4) Work-related pressure:
- a) can cause physical illness.
- b) is something I try to avoid.
- c) is a definite problem in business today.
- d) seldom causes me any discomfort.

5) I have generally been regarded as having:
- a) the ability to sell things.
- b) a good grasp of "what makes people tick."
- c) physical strength.
- d) emotional warmth.

6) To reach one's optimum level of success, one must:
- a) have luck on his or her side.
- b) be happy in his or her work.
- c) be willing to take risks.
- d) know the right people.

7) Personally, I:
- a) am dissatisfied with my current profession.
- b) have had a variety of life experiences.
- c) have strong business and sales skills.
- d) have not had much business experience.

8) A major factor in business success is:
   a) an appetite to learn more about what you do.
   b) a happy and stable personal life.
   c) physical stamina.
   d) extensive business experience.

9) I am *best* described as:
   a) an intelligent person.
   b) a highly verbal person.
   c) a hard-driving person.
   d) a person who can relate to other people.

10) A strong desire to learn is:
    a) a valuable asset, both personally and professionally.
    b) often necessary to advance in business.
    c) not very important once you complete school.
    d) uncommon in the business world.

11) When a superior tells me what to do, I:
    a) wish I had his job so I could give orders.
    b) often try to present a new, more efficient way of doing the task.
    c) secretly resent being ordered around.
    d) learn from the instructions and complete the task.

12) To succeed in business, it is often more important to be hard-working than to be a creative, talented person.
    a) I strongly agree.
    b) I agree.
    c) I disagree.
    d) I strongly disagree.

13) I have been *best* known for:
    a) getting involved in my community.
    b) having good general business knowledge and skills.
    c) being a good parent.
    d) my work experience with a large company organization.

14) As a business owner, it would be most important to me to:
    a) provide jobs to my family.
    b) be well thought of by my staff.
    c) be able to set my own work schedule.
    d) be closely aware of and prudent with my finances.

15) Work hours should be:
    a) as long as is needed.
    b) paid for, especially for the boss.
    c) flexible—long only when needed for special projects.
    d) equally divided among all employees.

16) A description of someone with a good chance to succeed in business is someone who:
    a) likes to regularly get away to help avoid stress.
    b) is always curious to learn more about doing her job.
    c) works best by himself.
    d) has a business degree from a top university.

For questions 17-30, pick the statement that best describes you.

17)   a) I have a strong affinity for sales.
       b) I am highly energetic.

18)   a) I have moderate experience in the type of business I would like to get into.
       b) I am a good direction-taker.

19)   a) I am a creative person.
       b) I am a good listener.

20)   a) I am a previous business owner.
       b) I am able to fully commit my finances to my business.

21)   a) I don't mind working long hours.
       b) I have strong corporate skills.

22)   a) I am a very careful, organized person.
       b) I am a people-oriented person.

23)   a) I am a charitable person.
       b) I am a diplomatic person.

24)   a) I am highly spontaneous.
       b) I am highly goal-directed.

25)   a) I am able to take charge of people.
       b) I am a quick decision-maker.

26)   a) I have some basic financial knowledge.
       b) I have previous management experience.

27)   a) I need to be in control.
       b) I can take directions from others.

28)   a) I have extensive business skills.
       b) I am always willing to do what it takes to get things done.

29)   a) I often use weekends to unwind after the work week.
       b) I am very resistant to stress.

30)   a) I have money in the bank.
       b) I am willing to do without if necessary.

31) For this question, circle the five following statements that are least like you:
       a) I am a slow starter.
       b) I am able to sell anything.
       c) I prefer to work by myself.
       d) I am interested in learning new skills.
       e) I would rather live spontaneously than set long-range goals.
       f) I thrive on stressful, busy, deadline situations.
       g) I work best by taking charge and issuing orders.
       h) I am rich in people skills.
       i) I prefer a large, corporate environment.
       j) I have a history of working long hours at favorite activities.

Scoring

For each answer you have chosen, give yourself the corresponding amount of points listed below:

1) a-0, b-4, c-0, d-2	18) a-1, b-2
2) a-2, b-0, c-4, d-0	19) a-1, b-2
3) a-4, b-0, c-2, d-1	20) a-1, b-2
4) a-0, b-0, c-1, d-4	21) a-2, b-1
5) a-4, b-2, c-0, d-0	22) a-1, b-2
6) a-0, b-2, c-4, d-0	23) a-1, b-2
7) a-0, b-2, c-4, d-0	24) a-1, b-2
8) a-4, b-1, c-0, d-3	25) a-2, b-1
9) a-1, b-0, c-2, d-4	26) a-2, b-1
10) a-4, b-2, c-0, d-0	27) a-1, b-2
11) a-0, b-2, c-0, d-4	28) a-1, b-2
12) a-4, b-3, c-0, d-0	29) a-1, b-2
13) a-0, b-4, c-2, d-1	30) a-2, b-1
14) a-1, b-0, c-0, d-4	31) a-1, b-0, c-1, d-0,
15) a-4, b-0, c-2, d-0	e-1, f-0, g-1, h-0, i-1,
16) a-0, b-4, c-1, d-1	j-0
17) a-2, b-1	

TOTAL POINTS POSSIBLE: 97

Ratings

97-80 points: A Prime Candidate. Congratulations! If you have answered the quiz questions frankly and received a score in this range, your personality traits, attitude, experience, and temperament are good matches with the attributes many franchisors say are found in their most successful franchisees. You likely have a well-defined desire to learn and a willingness to follow directions in the quest for your own success. If you are financially able to do so, I strongly suggest that you pursue becoming a franchisee. Good luck!

79-50 points: A Potential Candidate. Many of your traits are close to those found in top franchise candidates. However, you may not be *completely* committed to the concept of running a franchised outlet of someone else's business. Although you may be interested in becoming a franchisee, your quiz answers indicate you might have some differences in opinion as compared with more "traditional" candidates; perhaps you have a strong streak of independence or are more comfortable giving directions than taking them. If you can ascertain those areas in which you differ from the "model franchisee"—by reading the following section analyzing important traits—you may be able to determine if these are fundamental differences (which may mean that franchising is not for you) or are merely slight discrepancies. If the latter is true, you too could turn out to be a good franchisee candidate.

49-0 points: A Questionable Candidate. A low score on this test might simply indicate that you would be more comfortable and successful as an independent business owner or as an employee of an independent business or a large corporation. Becoming a franchisee is not for every personality type. You may be more independent and have a stronger business background than most franchisees. Rather than trying to squeeze your individual talents into a field for which you may not be suited, you should probably seek other opportunities. If you still feel you are strongly committed to becoming a franchisee, examine the choices you made on the test that differ from the suggested answers. Doing this can show you which areas in your personality or background you need to reassess to improve your chances at becoming a successful franchisee. Read on, and we will closely examine those traits and show you which ones are and aren't judged to be important to success as a franchisee.

The Most Important Franchisee Traits

The following were the most highly rated franchise traits by the respondents to the Francorp/DePaul survey. Most of the respondents judged each of the following characteristics to be "critical" to a franchisee's success.

1) Eagerness to Learn

More than three-quarters of the survey's respondents chose this trait as critical, making it the highest-rated and, one could conclude, the most important attribute many franchisors look for among prospective franchisees. This comes as little surprise since, in effect, franchising can be boiled down to two tasks: teaching and systemization. These words obviously oversimplify the matter, but the point is still valid. Franchisors teach their franchisees how to run the business (or, in the case of conversion franchises, franchisors teach their franchisees a modified and, presumably, an improved way of doing business). These "students" must and will—albeit naturally—repeat their lessons over and over as they serve their customers. Therefore, it follows that an eagerness to learn would serve a franchisee well. This eagerness to learn is not necessarily to be confused with having an education, although it is a definite advantage to have a high school education, and at least *some* amount of college can be helpful. Less than 10 percent of those franchisors replying said that some particular level of formal education was a critical requirement.

2) *Willingness to Work Long Hours*

The fact that more than two-thirds of all respondents identified this as a critical trait clearly underscores the point that there is no easy road to success in business ownership. Simply put, franchisees who want to succeed can expect to work long and hard hours to make their businesses successful, especially in the early days of running their units. In other words, you will have little or *no* staff to rely upon except, perhaps, unpaid family members—quite a different situation from the backgrounds of most corporate executives. Franchisors require this sort of devotion from their franchisees, and prospective franchisees who are willing and aware of this have a better chance of making it than those who may be less committed to taking on the newer, potentially larger workload—definitely a case of perspiration, not inspiration.

3) *Highly Developed "People Skills"*

Franchisees have to artfully and diplomatically deal with suppliers, employees, franchisor personnel, and, most importantly, their customers. To best do so, franchisees need to be able to express themselves, listen, and have patience in dealing with a variety of situations. Accordingly, franchisors look at the way you present yourself, the way you enumerate your skills, and the way you handle their questions. In other words, the franchisor will evaluate how you "sell" yourself. Again, this is a skill that can be learned—just notice how individuals who are at least somewhat outgoing and communicative are able to instill confidence in those around them. I cannot stress enough the need for an ability to listen. The good news is that this skill, as rare as it may be, can be taught. Remember—God gave us all two ears and only one mouth for good reason.

4) Sales Ability

Whether it is pizzas, pets, or paint jobs, every franchise sells something. While you need not be a master salesperson to survive or succeed as a franchisee, you will need at least some level of sales ability. In a way, the evaluation of this ability will likely start the instant you meet with a franchisor, including the way you present yourself, the way you enumerate your skills, and the way you handle their questions. In other words, the franchisor will evaluate how you "sell" yourself. Again, this is a skill that can be learned—just notice how many sales seminars are conducted every year.

5) Resistance to Stress

It's your twelfth straight hour working at your franchised outlet. The phone is ringing, a customer's baby is crying, an employee needs you to handle a dispute with an irate customer, and you're behind on getting your required paperwork filled out and sent to the franchisor's headquarters. A bad day? Sure, but it could be any day in the life of a new franchisee. You are likely to face some trying and stressful days (and nights), especially during the period before running your franchise becomes second nature. Can your temperament handle these situations? Can you focus on necessary tasks, no matter what distractions and/or deadlines accompany them? Franchisors know being a franchisee is often stressful, which is why they will want to know how well you handle stress. (This is another skill that can be learned, and probably should be by most businesspeople!)

6) Ability to Take Directions

Similar to "eagerness to learn" (yet with a subtle difference), this trait was rated as critical by more than half of those franchisors who responded to the survey. In franchising, faith and trust must be placed in the methods the franchisor has developed. Directions and requirements are not made capriciously, but rather to benefit the franchisee and the rest of the franchise system. Consequently, franchisees must be able to subordinate many of their personal opinions and desires to those of the franchisor. For example, an unyielding "my way or the highway" type of person who chafes at taking suggestions or orders is not a good candidate to become a successful franchisee.

7) *Having Money in Reserve*

More than 90 percent of respondents rated this trait as either critical or at least somewhat important to the success of a franchisee. This may contradict the common perception of a franchisee who has his "last dime" invested in his business (and, therefore, in himself), but it just makes good business sense. Yes, franchisors want their franchisees to be committed, both personally and financially, to the success of their units but they also want the franchisee to be financially able to weather any hard times, either early on in the life of a particular unit or during an uncontrollable economic downturn. A franchisee with some money in reserve will be better able to deal with any hard times that may be encountered.

The Least Important Franchisee Traits

The highly rated traits noted above give you a better idea of what most franchisors are looking for in franchisees, but, conversely, what traits are not important to franchisors? I have also identified those attributes, and some of them may surprise you. The following traits were judged to be *irrelevant* to a franchisee's potential for success by most of the franchisors who replied to the survey.

1) *Experience Working for a Big Company*

Nearly 85 percent of the respondents said this trait had nothing to do with whether a franchisee could be successful in their system (in comparison, only 2 percent rated this as being critical). While most franchisors have a number of franchisees who have bailed out (or been euphemistically "outplaced") of corporate life, in no way do these franchisors place much importance on this background.

2) *Previous Experience in the Franchisor's Field*

Most of the franchisors surveyed downplayed the importance of prior experience in their line of business. In fact, over the years we have seen many franchisors who would much prefer to deal with franchisees who have no experience in their field. The franchisors often feel that it is easier to train these novices than it is to retrain someone with preexisting ideas and habits (i.e., ideas and habits contrary to those of the franchisor).

3) Prior Business Ownership (or Lack Thereof)

This trait was posed as both a positive and a negative question. In the positive sense: "Are franchisees who have previously owned their own business more likely to be successful as a franchisee?" In the negative sense: "Are franchisees who have not previously owned their own business more likely to be successful as a franchisee?" Perhaps surprisingly, neither the first condition nor the second condition rated very highly among franchisors. With the obvious exception of conversion franchisees, franchisors are neither specifically looking for people who have owned their own businesses, nor are they systematically seeking to exclude these people. Franchisors feel that some level of prior business experience can be helpful, but the degree of this experience is far less important in the development of a successful franchisee than (for example) an eagerness to learn and an ability to follow directions.

4) Personal Situations (Age, Sex, and Marital/Family Status)

Conventional wisdom might dictate that most franchisors would prefer middle-aged, married males with a family as franchisees because, perhaps, members of this group are usually regarded as being responsible individuals with vested interests in succeeding (i.e., to support their families). However, respondents to this survey indicated that age, sex, marital status, and family situations meant little when it came to predicting future franchisee success. The percentage of respondents who considered these "irrelevant" were as follows: **Age**, 59 percent; **Sex**, 79 percent; **Marital Status**, 71 percent; and **Family Status**, 62 percent.

Also worthy of note are that these questions were not qualified. For example, the question simply inquired "If the sex of a franchisee matters," not if the franchisor preferred males over females or vice versa.

5) Financial Acumen

Did you often doze off during Accounting 101? Not to worry. The total of franchisor respondents who judged this characteristic to be either irrelevant or only somewhat important to a franchisee's success was more than 77 percent. Some knowledge of basic accounting and reporting conventions *can* be helpful, but whatever financial routines are needed will likely be taught by the franchisor, including standardized accounting, banking, and other financial procedures that will be part of the operating system provided. In general, franchisors are looking for enthusiastic, committed, quick learners, not necessarily CPAs.

Other traits that the survey inquired about were judged to be neither critical in the absolute sense, nor completely irrelevant by the franchisors who responded. These include general physical fitness, creativity, participation in community affairs, management experience (i.e., previously overseeing a staff, an outlet, or an entire business) or other specialized business skills, and a willingness to take risks.

Now that you know which traits are valued most by franchisors in successful franchisees—and which traits mean relatively little—you should have a clearer picture of where you stand in regard to them. You also have a better idea of why you scored the way you did on the quiz (whether it was a high or low score). Perhaps, especially if you were disappointed with your score, you could benefit from looking over the test questions again, analyzing your responses as they compare to what you now know to be important to a franchisor.

The Next Step

Now that you have a better idea of how you rate—personally and professionally—as a prospective franchisee, the next step on your journey is to begin evaluating franchises toward the ultimate decision of choosing a franchise organization with which to cast your lot. Of course, the franchisor that you choose must also choose *you*, but if you're pleased with your test score and if you feel the traits described above dovetail nicely with your personality and experiences, you have a good chance of appealing to many franchisors as a possible franchisee.

How to Buy a Franchise

Finding the "Perfect" Franchise

Remember the old adage, "if you give a person a fish, you feed him for a day, but if you teach a him to fish, you feed him for a lifetime?" Telling you which franchise you should buy would be like giving you a fish, and even with my experience and expertise in the field, by the time you read any individual suggestion(s) I could make...well, you know what happens to a fish past its prime—it rots.

On the other hand, if I show you how to intelligently weigh all of the factors involved in making the choice best suited to your abilities and background, I have instead shared my fishing experience. After all, it *should* be your decision—my goal is simply to better prepare you to make it. So bait up your hook, and prepare to cast your line into the well-stocked waters of franchising.

At this point, you might be thinking, "But I already know what franchise I want to buy." If so, fine, I am not trying to talk you out of anything, but I suggest you read on to see the important component parts that should go into such a decision. It may either reinforce your choice or help you to reevaluate it.

How Not to Become a Franchisee

Before examining the factors that go into a well-rounded decision on how to become a franchisee, I need to run through approaches or attitudes I feel can be detrimental to the process. Here then, are four ways *not* to become a franchisee.

1) Do Not Rely on Brokers

While I *strongly* suggest you solicit the advice of experts (such as lawyers, accountants, and qualified consultants) at the appropriate times, I do not feel your best interests are served by abdicating your research or your decision making responsibilities to others. There are a variety of brokers and agents who may or may not have your best interests in mind when it comes to making a business decision—so why entrust your future to their hands? The field of franchise consulting has many well-established companies and individuals, but for the most part these consultants best help people become *franchisors*. I heartily endorse use of reputable consultants for that process. As for becoming a franchisee, it's *your* money, *your* life, and *your* future—be sure to make it *your* decision!

2) Do Not Look to Get Rich Quick

I feel this is important enough to repeat: *The perception of franchising as a "license to print money" arose during the first franchising boom of the 1960s and was reinforced during the last decade or so. But as any experienced person knows, there is no sure thing in business. Remember, when a person with experience meets a person with money, the person with money usually gets experience—and vice versa!* Yes, franchising has an enviable record of success, but it's not magic. By making a carefully informed decision and backing it up with dedicated hard work, you can make a successful go of franchising. Just understand that, as in any business endeavor, your success is not *guaranteed*.

3) Do Not Try to Get into Franchising "On the Cheap"

It takes time and money to take to get into franchising. Perhaps I should have said, "it takes time and money to get into franchising *intelligently."* Choosing a franchise is a complex decision that requires a *critical* period of time and a *certain* amount of money. Thinking you can do it cheaply by cutting corners and collapsing time frames can be potentially disastrous.

4) The Right Way to Choose a Franchise

As with any important venture, as you enter franchising, you need to identify your desires and goals. After taking the test in Chapter 5, you should have a better sense of whether becoming a franchisee is right for you—but there's more you need to consider. What sort of fields do you know or are interested in? Do you want to be in a field you know and have experience in, or do you want to try something new? Do you want to simply, in effect, buy yourself a job? Do you want to establish something you can pass on to your children? Do you want to be a sort of mini-entrepreneur, owning more than one franchise or an entire franchise territory? Are you interested more in the long- or the short-term? Do you want a proven franchise or more of a long shot with a potentially larger payoff?

Knowing the answers will help you narrow your choices. As you examine various industries or individual franchises, you will have personal objectives against which to measure them. At this point however, your single most important consideration should be how much risk you are willing to take. (In later stages of consideration, financial matters of investment, rates of return, potential income, etc., are another group of very important considerations.)

The Risk Continuum

The very fact that you are considering buying a franchise means you want, among other things, less risk than is involved in starting an independent business.

You are looking at getting into a business with the advantages of a proven operating system, ongoing support, and wide ranging (perhaps even national) advertising promotion. Though given the generally less risky nature of franchising, varying levels of risk do exist, and tied to these levels are different risk/reward payoffs! This relationship can be illustrated by the chart below.

The three points on this continuum represent convenient touch-stones in the intertwined relationship of *risk*, *cost*, and *return*. Countless gradations could represent variances in any individual element or in all three, but to give you a general idea of the elements involved, I will describe three demarcations.

1) Low Risk, High Cost, Low Return

To minimize your risk (but maximize your cost), you could buy an existing, operating, proven franchise outlet. Even if you succeed, you will not make a fortune, but your likelihood of making money *at all* will be significantly increased. How much should you expect to make, given your level of low risk? Considering the probable cost of such a blue-chip franchise, you are likely to have to lay out a substantial amount of cash, or take on a substantial amount of debt. Of course, if that route is your choice, franchising is really secondary. You are just buying a business that happens to be a franchise. The only difference between doing that and buying any existing business is that perhaps you can feel more confident that last year's performance will be duplicated next year and the year after, thanks to support from the franchisor. If this is your chosen course, call franchisees in your own backyard to see if they are interested in selling. Of course, the franchisors will also have their say in this matter. Many franchisors retain the right of first refusal over any franchise resales, making it potentially more difficult to buy an existing franchise.

2) Medium Risk, Medium Cost, Medium Return

A more risky course of action would be to buy a franchise that has less of a blue-chip aura—with an accompanying reduction in price. The three elements that generally establish an individual franchise outlet's level of risk are: the relative newness of *industry*, *franchise*, and *market* (location). So in general, a medium-risk/cost/return franchise would have some elements of relative newness to one or more of those three categories.

"Gray area" solutions (as opposed to the black and white solutions to simple questions like, "What happens if I do not pay the store's electric bill?") are substantially more subjective in nature. A "gray area" issue, for example, would be, "What is riskier—a brand-new franchise in an established industry in an emerging market, or an established franchise in an emerging industry in a new market?" In general, "venture capital-like" companies will be riskier than blue-chip companies—with a corresponding drop in price and *potentially* higher return.

3) High Risk, Low Cost, High Return

Following the continuum to its logical end, I come to the riskiest and, potentially, most lucrative type of franchise (in other words, these franchises represent a relatively high degree of newness in all three categories). Theoretically of course, the riskiest franchise would be a completely new franchise, in a completely new industry, in a completely new market.

If you're up to the challenge of this kind of franchise and make calls to see if entire franchise territories are available, even if you had not considered taking on a franchise territory (which makes you sort of a hybrid between a franchisee and franchisor), and if you're willing to take on a high level of risk, the rewards of territory development can be more than worth it.

For example, when Blockbuster Video started out, it was a considerable risk. They were stocking more than five times the number of tapes than regular video stores were, and it was capital-intensive and expensive for an unproven concept. But those who bought territories early on benefited greatly (some to the tune of up to ten times their initial investment) by developing and eventually selling the territory back to the parent company.

Once you have an idea where you want to fall on the risk continuum, you can assess the other major factor that will likely steer your decision in the early stages: *emotion*.

Emotion: The Immeasurable Factor

Now that I have established the risk/return relationship, imagine a two-dimensional graph, with risk/return (from low to high) as the vertical axis. I say *"imagine"* because this is not a graph you can actually plot lines on, but you can learn from it.

The reason for the imaginary status of this graph is that when considering a franchise, the horizontal axis would be labeled *"emotion,"* an immeasurable and unpredictable factor. It's simply impossible to plot emotion on a linear scale. No matter what logic dictates, there will always be someone who says, "Risk, 'schmisk.' I want a pizza franchise because I've always wanted to spin that dough in the air," or "I want that lawn care franchise because I've always wanted to work outside all day," or whatever it is you have always wanted to do.

Basically, it can be said there are two kinds of potential franchisees: (1) those interested in getting into the franchising business, and (2) those interested in getting into the chicken or oil-change or *whatever* business. This is not to say that one is better than the other. Looking at the entire field of franchising may be more logical, but I realize the emotional attraction of one particular field or franchise often can be strong.

My brother, John, bought a Physicians Weight Loss Center franchise after he lost sixty pounds as a customer at his local franchise. He did not know diet centers or weight-loss plans, but he did know he lost more than 20 percent of his total body weight, so he got into the business. The results were disastrous, and this is not an isolated example.

Executives in Donald Boroian's company, Francorp, recently had occasion to talk to executives from Popeye's Famous Fried Chicken in New Orleans. They have some seven hundred units and had recently acquired Church's Fried Chicken as well, with another 1,200 or so units. They were asked about the common denominators of their typical franchisees. The response: "We've got doctors, lawyers, bankers, families, husbands and wives, young professionals, etc., but the real common factor is most of them were first interested in becoming franchisees because they like the chicken." Popeye's also said a recent franchise of theirs was a perfect example of this phenomenon. This gentleman is a doctor who went to college in New Orleans. He liked the chicken back then, but his current practice is in a town without a Popeye's. He missed it and said, "I guess I'm gonna have to buy a franchise in order to have this chicken." So he did! Such is the power of emotion in the franchise-buying process.

The Danger of Liking the Chicken

Early in a franchise program, many franchisees tend to be customers of the particular business. The scenario is fairly straightforward: the customer is happy with the product or service, makes an inquiry as to its availability, and ends up purchasing a franchise. Oftentimes, risk/return decisions are not huge factors in these purchases—the customer simply likes the business, assumes other people will like it, and buys in. Perhaps I have you thinking about some business that you frequent and wonder, "Do they franchise?" or "Is that franchise available in my area?" The only way to find out is to *ask!*

However, there is a danger of falling in love with your product: You love this chicken, but will everyone else? Or "I love this pizza," but is the market saturated (in your area or nationwide—whatever market you're looking at)? Do not fall into the trap of romanticizing the business beyond its actual proportions. Remember, it's a business transaction. You're buying a franchise, not a pizza or a T-shirt or a service you like. Are there enough *other* people who will like it? Is the market growing or shrinking? You like the chicken, sure. But, to put it bluntly, do you like the chicken enough to eat it for *every* meal if your franchise is not making money?

This reminds me of the old joke about the banker who said, "I only lend money to liquor stores, because I know in the worst case I can drink my way out of the problem!"

Emotion versus Logic

As I said, risk/return is highly measurable and emotion is immeasurable. In the best-case scenario (or at least the most logical scenario), if emotion is removed from the buying process, you can choose the type of franchise that's best for your desired level of risk/return.

Logical as you may be, however, you can never fully remove emotion from a decision that large. Let's face it, many of life's major decisions have little to do with pure logic. For example, if you looked at getting married and having children in a strictly logical manner, you'd say, "It costs too much and it's too much hassle. Can I change my lifestyle that much?" But emotionally, it's "I love you, let's get married, let's buy a house, let's have kids." We know that marriages fail, houses cost too much, and having kids puts a strain on your time and money, but based on emotional appeal, we do these things and will keep doing them.

My goal here is to give you the analytical tools to work things out for yourself when it comes to choosing a franchise. I know you're still going to add your own emotions into the mix, but if you know the score, and if you consider the details logically as well as emotionally, you can at least minimize your chances of failure. In other words, do not be afraid to let your emotions come into play, but be aware that you're doing it and do not let your ultimate decision be *purely* emotional. Your goal should be to strike that delicate balance between "This is the amount of risk I'm comfortable with" and "I like the chicken!"

Furthermore, as the process progresses, you will need to become even more analytical. There will come a time you will need to weigh your choices from a standpoint of investment (of money and time) and return on that investment. Again, I will help you to best make that decision by highlighting the factors you should be considering.

Where Logic and Emotion Meet

If you were to approach the concept of picking a franchise in the most logical way possible, you would first choose the industry, and then you would narrow down available franchises within that industry.

As a matter of course, this rarely happens. It is much more common for potential franchisees to look at franchises in a number of different industries. This is a *horizontal* search, cutting across various franchises in various industries, rather than a *vertical* search of franchises within one industry.

Ironically, if you feel you "do not know where to start" when choosing a franchise, you're more likely to follow the logical course of total horizontal research. If you do know where to start, it may be because you have not fully considered the range of options available to you.

Of course, this phenomenon is not unique to franchising. Business brokers will tell you they often advertise bars or liquor stores, because they bring the people in. People think, "Oh yeah, I'd like to run a bar"—they romanticize the concept a bit. But when they come in to talk to the broker, they usually end up buying something else entirely. These people are also looking horizontally, and the broker plays on the appeal of the bar or liquor store to get them in the door—a "hook" if you will.

Also amazing is how many knowledgeable businesspeople look at franchising *horizontally* rather than vertically. An experienced franchisor who was being bought out of his share of a multimillion dollar franchise business came up to me at a party and said, "I'm going to have some cash after this deal. Which industry in franchising do you think is hot right now?" He's in the *franchising business*, and he does not care which industry he gets into—he just wants to know what is hot!

Strangely, in the horizontal search, the paths of the shrewd and the emotional cross. The shrewd businessperson does not care about the industry she is getting into as long as she makes money. The emotional person also does not care about the industry she is getting into—she just wants the franchise she has "always wanted." This does not guarantee that either one of them is going to be successful (though shrewdness would have to be awarded the inside track), but I'd have to admit that if they both fall, one of them is going to have a heck of a lot more fun doing it than the other one!

Establishing the Candidates

When you reach this point in your search, you should have a good idea of your general objectives, where you stand on the risk continuum, whether you have an emotional attachment toward any particular industry or individual franchise, and, with the assistance of some savvy research, which industries seem the most promising. The next step is to identify which specific industry (or industries) and/or franchise (or franchises) you are going to pursue. Basically, you are now going to shift your focus from broad industry trends to individual industries or businesses you might like to work in. If you have had your heart set on a particular franchise all along, you should have a bit more of an objective idea on how its industry stacks up.

The Resources

To assist you in assembling a list of industries and franchises to consider, there are two important resources that I suggest you employ.

1) Franchise Source Guides

The best place to begin your list is through a book listing the majority of franchises available in all categories. One of the best books of this type is *The Sourcebook of Franchise Opportunities* by Bond & Bond publishers. Other sources, less complete in their scope, include the *Franchise Opportunities Handbook*, produced annually by the International Franchise Association (IFA) of Washington, DC, and an assortment of magazine-like handbooks available at many bookstores and newsstands. The listings in these books typically include the name, address, and phone number of the franchisor, when the company was founded or began franchising, how many franchises and company owned outlets the franchisor has (and perhaps how many states these outlets are in), the franchise fee, and a range of capital requirements. Perhaps the *two most important* facts to consider when actually assembling your list are whether the company is actively seeking franchisees and, if so, in what areas of the country they are seeking them.

Those last two may seem like obvious points, but they can prevent you from wasting time considering options that really are not open to you. Some established franchisors are granting new franchises only to their current franchisees. Others may not be seeking franchisees in areas where you currently live or would be willing to relocate to—meaning this information should be a vital part of your screening process.

2) Franchise Trade Shows

Another way to gather (or refine) list-building information is to visit franchise trade shows, particularly those sponsored by the IFA. These shows are held frequently at hotels, exposition centers, and other convention facilities.

For a nominal fee (around $3 to $5 dollars, to cover a portion of the operating expenses), the public can browse thirty to seventy booths of exhibiting franchisors. The method of presentation varies from franchisor to franchisor. Some use videos, others have teams of salespeople, but the basic concept remains that they are attempting to both impress you with their franchise and qualify you somewhat as a potential franchisee (i.e., determine if you are serious about getting into their business, whether you can afford it, or if you are just browsing). If they feel you are qualified, they will endeavor to take your name and address and perhaps give you a franchise brochure. Aggressive franchisors will follow up later with a phone call. Many franchisors take your address rather than hand out the brochures directly since these brochures are usually expensive to produce, and it is not cost-effective to just pass out piles of these to prospects who may not be genuinely interested.

I strongly suggest that you attend at least one trade show (especially one sponsored by the IFA), but I must add a few caveats to this recommendation:

1) Do your general book research before you attend trade show.
2) Call the IFA for a list of franchisors attending the show you will be going to, and then check them in whichever book you have, so you are familiar with their background.
3) Bring the book with you so you can be immediately acquainted with important facts about any particular franchisor (such as its age, its franchise fee, the areas in which it is seeking franchises, etc.) before you talk to its representatives. You'll get more out of a trade show if you know who is going to be there, what their requirements are, and who you might be interested in talking to before you actually talk to them.

For more information, contact one of the following resources:

- International Franchise Association, Washington, DC, (202) 628-8000, fax: (202) 628-0812.
- The Overseas Private Investment Corp., Washington, DC, (202) 336-8799, fax: (202) 336-8700. Offers project financing, political risk insurance, and investor services.

- U.S. Department of Commerce, International Trade Administration, Washington, DC, (202) 482-2867, fax: (202) 482-4821. Offers Best Markets survey and access to district offices.
- Political Risk Services, East Syracuse, NY, (315) 431-0511, fax: (315) 431-0200. Offers the International Country Risk Guide.
- Franchise Business USA, Elmsford, NY, (914) 347-6735, fax: (914) 347-5012. Offers information on international franchise business development.
- Sibley International Corp., Washington, DC, (202) 833-9588, fax: (202) 775-9416. Specializes in international franchise business development.
- Welsh Bleck International Inc., Spokane, WA, (509) 624-7088. Franchise market research and consulting firm.

What Franchise Brochures Are and How to Get Them

Franchise brochures are the basic initial information and sales vehicles used to promote franchises to prospective franchisees. In the best of cases, they are creatively produced, written in laymen's terms (easy on the jargon, so as not to confuse the prospect), full of upbeat statistics, and usually illustrated with color photography, graphics, and perhaps charts.

The brochure's mission is to educate you on three things (in ascending order of importance): (1) franchising in general, (2) the market for the franchise's particular industry, and (3) the individual franchise itself. While franchise brochures are usually informative pieces, they are also infused with a decent helping of "sizzle" (as in the classic advertising adage, "Sell the sizzle, not the bacon").

Once you have created your list, call or write the franchisor's offices requesting information about their franchising programs, or, as noted above, you can leave your name and address with a franchisor at a trade show. Either way, you should hear from the franchisor quickly. Franchise brochures are an important early step in the selling process, and franchisors are not likely to delay getting their material to an eager audience. If they *do* take an inordinately long time to respond to your request, either they are swamped with requests, big enough not to care about interested prospects or sales candidates, or just plain inept. Realize this and govern yourself accordingly.

How to Read a Franchise Brochure

They say you can't judge a book by its cover, and that's usually true. Even if you receive a franchise brochure that's only somewhat attractive, read it with an open mind. Many young franchisors have more to offer in the way of potential than in money to spend on a brochure. However, if the brochure's design, writing, or overall quality is noticeably substandard, so might be the franchisor. In most cases, brochures will contain many (if not all) of the following features.

1) A Snappy Cover Blurb and Introduction

Franchise brochures are like any other sales/advertising vehicle: they want to grab your attention early and motivate you to read on. To that end, they usually start out with a bang on the cover and in the intro, often establishing a "clever" theme that will carry through the entire piece (e.g., using the Hollywood terms *four-star, box office success,* and *strong supporting cast* to describe a video rental franchise, sporting terms for a sports memorabilia franchise, etc.).

2) Explanation of the Concept

This section is the meat of the brochure, telling you about the franchise's general business concept, its point(s) of difference over its competitors (both franchised and nonfranchised), how its operating system works, and the special requirements, if any, needed to run the franchise, such as previous experience in the particular industry or various professional qualifications. Also in this section, statistics supporting franchising in general will likely be presented, as may quotes or case histories of successful franchisees.

3) Analysis of the Market/Industry and the Franchise's Niche Therein

I'm not trying to sound cynical, but you can probably guess that this section will tell you that the widget industry is booming. Which is not to say that this unfailing cheerleading is a necessarily bad thing. If you're going to put your future on the line with an XYZ Widget franchise, it's reassuring to know that there is a future. The best-written and produced brochures include useful footnoted quotes on industry or franchisor statistics and trends. You can learn more by following up on these quotes and tracking down the magazine or newspaper articles quoted. This, however, is only the case in the best examples. Franchise brochures usually use more loosely attributed quotes and facts (e.g., "Newsweek says this industry is booming!").

4) Background of the Company and/or Its Principal Personnel

This usually interesting section will provide historical background on the company, if there is any, and/or a capsule biography of the founder(s) or other principal personnel (if it is pertinent and if they are still with the company). Basically, whichever story is more cogent and/or compelling will get the biggest play. If the company is fairly new, for example, but its founder is well-known in her or his field, the coverage will focus more on the founder than on the company.

5) List and Explanation of the Franchisor's Advantages

This section tells you what you can expect to get from this franchise if you sign on as a franchisee. A known name, full training, a proven system (perhaps including proprietary computer software or various equipment), national or regional advertising, and ongoing support are among the advantages offered by most franchisors and described in detail in this section of the brochure. Also, for those not necessarily "converted" to franchising yet, the general benefits of it as a business system are usually also summarized.

6) Conclusion and Call to Action

The brochure usually wraps up with a conclusion that briefly reviews the franchise's concept and benefits and then challenges the reader to take the next step in the process filling out the brief "evaluation form" (sort of a preapplication) often included with the brochure or by calling the franchisor's sales department. Bearing all this in mind, sometimes what is not included in a brochure can tell you as much as what is included.

Where's the Beef?

Since all franchise brochures aim to project a positive, feel-good image of the franchises they describe, it can be difficult to get a well-rounded picture of a franchise simply by reading a brochure. As you would expect, the franchise brochure is not going to address negatives—be they the franchisor's shaky image, the uncertain state of the industry, or the franchisor's plummeting market share. But by carefully reading a brochure and noting *what is not included* in it, you can often discover which areas you need to investigate more deeply if you are to pursue this particular franchisor.

An example: You're reading the brochure of a longtime (but not superstar-level) franchisor. You notice that it includes neither company history nor founder/principal personnel profiles. Perhaps modesty has prevailed at this franchisor. More likely, it has undergone a management shake-up, a semi-recent change of direction, or some other change that makes its history a moot point. This need not be a bad thing (perhaps the old direction *was* failing), but it is something you *should* be aware of and something you *should* investigate.

Similarly, if you find a brochure to be lacking in solid facts about the franchisor's field (and its place in that field), its business system, or its advantages to franchisees, you have to ask yourself, "What are they leaving out and why?" There's probably a reason this material has been omitted—and it's probably not a flattering one. Again, follow up with your own research. You may find your doubts erased or find that this franchisor needs to be erased from your list!

Further Evaluating the Candidates

Okay. You have read your brochures, probably crossed a few more candidates off your list, and you're almost ready for the next step: beginning the actual buying process by visiting franchisors. Since this can be an expensive proposition (relatively speaking, it is not expensive when compared to what you will be investing in your eventual franchise), you want to make sure you have cut out any deadwood before you start. There's a little more research to do.

First, take a closer, long-term look at the industry (or industries) your "possibles" are in. Are they up, down, stable? What do the forecasters say about the future? And try to find out why things are up, down, or static. Could it be temporary? Caused by internal or external forces? How will the industry fare the next time the economy changes?

Next, do more research on the individual franchises you are considering. Are they selling more or fewer franchises than they have in the past? If the answer is more, is this true growth or just a temporary upswing? Ask the same question about gross sales at the franchised units? Are they growing? Why? Simply because of a recent price increase or due to actual, steady growth?

I suggest that you also read up on *general trend analysis* in any of John Naisbitt's books. His original book, **Naisbitt Megatrends,** is a good place to begin. How will the new directions charted in those books (or other future-oriented sources) affect the industries and franchises you are considering? Which franchises will benefit from likely coming trends?

Which will be harmed by them, perhaps even be made obsolete? Are the target customer groups of a particular franchise a growing or shrinking demographic? Does its prime customer base cut across socioeconomic lines? Will there be more or fewer people that desire or need its service in the coming years?

The bottom line is this: The world (and the people and businesses in it) constantly undergoes change—sometimes quickly, other times slowly, sometimes for the better, other times for the worse. What you have to try to perceive, as best as you are able, is how these changes may affect the business(es) you are considering getting into.

All the knowledge and research you accumulate will help you when the time comes to make your ultimate decision, but before you do, I am going to share a little more of our accumulated knowledge with you and advise you on some characteristics of franchises that you should avoid. Think of it as the final fine-tuning of your list before you make the great leap of actually visiting franchisors and evaluating these franchises as purely financial investments.

Franchises to Avoid: The Final Tuning

Following are some warning signs to look for that may indicate that an existing franchise may not be a particularly good choice. My advice is generally to avoid the following.

1) Franchisors with a Single Fad Product

Some of the entries are this type. Fresh muffins may be a great hit for six months or a year, but how many muffins can the public eat before they get tired of them? Not to mention, "How long will it be before the cookie shop next door adds them as a sideline?"

2) Labor-Intensive or Widely Unautomated Franchises

If you have followed business and societal trends for the last few years, you know how difficult it has become to attract (marginally above) minimum-wage workers. As the pool of these workers continues to dwindle and the competition for them among employers increases, many franchisees are going to find their labor costs increasing dramatically. Instead of being saddled with a franchise that relies too heavily on this uncertain pool of workers, you will want a franchise operating system that minimizes your overhead costs, and, at the same time, minimizes the potential for human error. If the business you like intrinsically requires a staff, look for a franchise system that keeps that staff as small as possible—hence, your labor expense—which could be the franchise's competitive edge.

Nevertheless, a business that you can run as a one-person shop needs proven systems in place, be they mechanical, computerized, or otherwise efficient. Because if it's all up to you and your skills, why in the world would you be paying the franchisor to allow you to do this? Remember, you are buying a franchise, and logically, you have every right to expect the franchisor to provide you with value for your money—in this case, the value of an established, effective, and efficient business system. Just look at the value provided by a McDonald's franchise!

3) Franchisors with Legal Problems or a Multitude of Failed Franchisees

Have you uncovered stories of legal problems in the background of a particular franchisor? Has it recently lost a significant number of franchisees? As you can well imagine, these are not good signs. If these problems were in the fairly distant past, perhaps the franchisor has turned things around. If the problems are more recent, watch out, because you may be about to step into a viper's nest of hassles. Although the franchisor has to fully disclose this sort of information in later stages of discussion, you are better off knowing it now—all the more reason to do thorough research.

4) Franchisors Whose Unit Sales Have Been Declining or Are below Industry Averages

Is the "bloom" off the rose? Did this franchisor once rule its market but has slipped in the face of growing competition? If so, maybe you should be looking at one of those competitors instead. Also, are its sales, even if they *are* growing, below the average for its industry? If everyone else is making more money in this field, what is this franchisor doing wrong? Remember, for your best shot at success, you do not want a business whose performance is average, or even good—you want *superior*. It is like the old story about the experienced jockey who is asked the best way to win the Kentucky Derby. "Ride the fastest horse," he simply replied. You do not want just any old nag—you want the fastest horse!

5) Franchisors with Limited Ongoing Support or Advertising

Again, what are you paying for? A percentage of your sales will be going to royalties, and you have a right to expect service and support for your money. Franchisors who provide little more than a trademark and a kind word should definitely be avoided.

Why Franchises Fail

As you should realize by now, franchising is not a "sure thing." The U.S. Department of Commerce estimates an annual failure rate for franchised businesses much lower than the failure rate for new, independent businesses (estimated by various sources as ranging from 30 to 90 percent during the first five years of operation). But the greater success rate will be of little comfort to you if you find yourself among the small minority who *do* fail.

The fact of the matter is that despite the proven record of franchising, some franchises do fail—and some of these are even franchises of well-established, "superstar" franchisors. The precise reasons for franchise failures can be as many as the outlets itself, but some are more common than others. Here are eleven common reasons why franchises fail:

1) Poor business concept or system
2) Poor location
3) Weak management
4) Incompatibility of franchisee skills with those needed to successfully run the franchise
5) Poor profit potential
6) Too much competition
7) Territory too small
8) Poor support by the franchisor
9) Fraud on the part of the franchisor
10) Lack of working capital
11) Unforeseen disasters

1) Poor Business Concept or System

If a franchise's basic concept or operating system is fundamentally flawed, no amount of hard work on the part of a franchisee will likely overcome this handicap. It is therefore vitally important to fully research a franchise's history and current status before you buy. If it's a long-time franchisor, has it had a rash of recent franchisee failures? If it's a new franchisor or it's expanding into a new area, conduct an informal survey of friends and associates. Ask them if they need or desire the product or service the franchise is offering. No matter the "good deal" you can get by becoming, for example, the first franchisee of the Acme Pet Psychiatrist chain, it is not going to be worth your time and money if not enough people want to purchase your services. The same can be true of businesses that are not proven, such as a business tied too heavily to a fad that eventually fades.

2) Poor Location

The old quip about "location, location, location" being the three most important considerations in determining a retailer's success is at least partly true. While a good or "perfect" location cannot assure a franchise of success, a bad location can doom even the most promising of franchises. What's a bad location? It can range from being located in a run-down or otherwise dangerous neighborhood to being in a brand-new shopping mall away from established traffic patterns. Fast food franchises can usually survive in either strictly residential or business areas (although in areas with different peak times of traffic, they may have different peak hours and even different operating hours). Housewares or business equipment franchises, on the other hand, would likely do best in an area close to their respective target customers. If a particular franchisor has shown success in helping franchisees find and secure locations, this can be very valuable assistance, even if there is an additional charge for it.

3) Weak Management

In most cases, franchisees need to be actively involved in the day-to-day operation of their franchises. This is a major reason most franchisors will not sell franchises to "absentee investors," who buy the unit but do not actively participate in running it. For example, I would conservatively guess that there are literally *thousands* of established professionals who would love to buy a McDonald's franchise as an investment, but McDonald's will not sell to absentee investors. Their attitude is "You want a McDonald's franchise? Fine, but you'll have to quit your job and work the store." Of course, huge franchise investments such as hotels are an exception. Franchisees of these types of businesses often just provide the money, then hire a staff or management company to run the business for them.

4) Incompatibility of Franchisee Skills with Those Needed to Successfully Run the Franchise

In other words, can a franchisee administrator or a manager do the job of a salesman? The most successful franchisees have at least *some* sales ability, are people-oriented, do not mind hard work, and are eager to learn. The most meticulous franchisors look for these traits in potential franchisees, as well as other specific characteristics that they know from experience are necessary or beneficial in their line of business. But if a franchisor does not care and a franchisee fools himself into believing he has what it takes, the result can be a failed franchise. If you do not like or cannot do the particular work that a particular franchise requires, it is not the right franchise for you, no matter how attractive the investment.

5) Poor Profit Potential

Though obvious, this point needs to be stated. If a franchised business has to produce huge sales numbers from the day it opens just to cover the costs of goods, salaries, and royalties, where is your profit margin going to come from? There are some exceptions (such as low overhead and one- or two-person franchises, especially in the janitorial field), but in general, businesses with inherently small profit margins, low sales figures, or high prices (and low volume) are usually not good candidates for success in franchising. You will want to make more money on your investment than you could by simply putting your money in a bank or government bond!

6) Too Much Competition

This ties in with location. That is, although several different types of fast food restaurants on the same street can help each other by increasing customer traffic in the entire area, *too many* restaurants on the same street can hurt the entire group by diluting the customer base. How many is too many? When is local competition a threat rather than just a source of healthy rivalry? Franchisors should have some answers, backed up with research and experience, to these questions. If they don't, be careful. The strength of being part of a franchise does not guarantee success, and there have been plenty of examples of even well-known franchises faring poorly in competition against locally popular businesses in the same field. For example, Domino's Pizza experienced years of difficulty cracking the Chicago market because that city boasts a large number of long-established pizza parlors which also deliver. They have carved out individual niches and engendered fierce loyalties. There are also several excellent regional franchises in the Chicago area which resist inroads in their market areas by national chains.

7) Territory Too Small

If the area from which a franchise is supposed to draw its primary customers is too small to provide an adequate base, the franchise can be endangered before it even opens. Of course, some franchise territories are limited to the site of the outlet itself, but most franchises allow a general radius in which another corporate-owned or franchised outlet of the same chain will be located. It can be hard enough to compete against other chains and local businesses, but a franchisee forced to compete with its own franchisor has an uphill battle indeed. The importance of territory size becomes even more critical when your franchise is a service-oriented one that needs to make sales calls within its assigned area.

8) Poor Support by the Franchisor

Training, advertising, general publicity, contracts for supplies that have been negotiated with the power of multiple buying, ongoing assistance—these are the sorts of things for which franchisees pay royalties to franchisors. I will examine royalties and other financial and investment-related aspects of becoming a franchisee later; but if these services are lacking while the royalties are still being paid, a franchise will face an uphill battle.

9) Fraud on the Part of the Franchisor

Fraud occurs less frequently than it did during the early, less regulated years of franchising, but every so often you hear or read about a franchise that has folded due to its franchisor's financial or operational vagaries. The franchisees of these failed systems either go under, attempt to operate as a renamed independent, or (in rare cases) are snapped up as franchisees of a competing franchise.

10) Lack of Working Capital

Franchisors generally consider it more important for a franchisee to have at least some money in reserve than for a franchisee to have his or her "last dime" in the business. Sure, complete financial commitment is desirable, but it is even more important for a franchisee to be able to weather any financial storms that may appear during the first months of a franchise's operation. Lack of liquid capital to cover these sorts of emergencies has doomed many a franchisee to failure.

11) Unforeseen Disasters

Even though this is not a category that you can consciously try to avoid or otherwise prepare for, it can be a considerable cause of franchisee failure. For example, a Dunkin' Donuts near Donald Boroian's office in a Chicago suburb was basically put *out of operation* for about five months when the road it was on was closed for widening. Another good example of an *unanticipated* problem occurred in the late 1970s when McDonald's outlets in and around Atlanta were rumored to be serving burgers with worms ground into the meat (the rumor later spread throughout the country). Of course, the rumor was completely untrue. For one thing, as Ray Kroc quickly pointed out, worms cost more per pound than beef. But the rumor did negatively affect the chain's sales throughout the Southeast for a few months until the charges were proven unfounded and the damage somewhat controlled. It is quite possible that a more damaging rumor aimed at a weaker franchise could cause such sales falloffs as to induce individual—or even chainwide—failures. Unforeseen occurrences can also include "acts of God," such as tornadoes, earthquakes, and hurricanes. Insurance can help in these instances, but the setback can still ruin unprepared (or *under*prepared) franchisees. I hate to sound pessimistic, but it is always a good idea to think of the worst things that could happen to your business, and then, whenever possible, prepare for these potential calamities as best you can.

Sufficiently warned? Well, I wouldn't want you to accuse me of making franchising sound like a simple stroll down Easy Street! Seriously, however, franchising can be an excellent form of business for the right people. Bear in mind many of the reasons for failure I enumerated also apply to nonfranchised businesses and that your franchisor should help you anticipate and deal with most of these potential danger areas.

Now that you've fully researched your choices of potential franchisors, you're ready for the next logical step—learning more about the franchisor (or franchisors) in which you are most interested.

Finding Out about the Franchisor

To make the best, most informed decision regarding a franchisor that you can, you have to know as much as you can find out about the franchisor. This can be primarily divided into four parts:

1) Visiting the franchisor
2) Obtaining and analyzing documents and forms
3) Talking to current franchisees
4) Looking at earnings claims

1) Visiting the Franchisor

As I have said, it takes time and money to become a franchisee—not simply to buy a franchise, but to investigate your options. You should allot sufficient time to visit at least three franchisors. You should also spend time visiting individual franchises. Of course, this could mean spending travel money as well.

At the franchisor's headquarters, you will likely do the following: meet the franchisor's upper-level management, see its corporate facility, receive important legal documents, be asked to fill out an application (if one hadn't been sent to you previously), and generally get to know more about the franchisor. Make no mistake about it, you are also going to be evaluated, and if you are acceptable to the franchisor, you are also going to be more or less continuously and subtly persuaded of the advantages of becoming a franchisee of this franchisor's system.

Also, if you are married, it is to your best interest to bring your spouse along on this visit. Even if he or she isn't going to directly work in or with your franchise, buying a franchise is still a big commitment, and is worthy of consideration by both members of a life partnership. Sure, it's a full-blown visit (if the franchisor is located in a distant city, it may cost you around $1,000 in transportation and accommodations for two), but in general, I think it's worth it. You're about to invest your life and your future in this venture (not to mention substantially more than $1,000)—so don't be penny-wise and pound-foolish. Also, your willingness to invest some initial time and money to make this visit shows the franchisor you are serious and are ready to fully commit even more time and money to the right franchisor. If the franchisor is savvy and is truly interested in you as a franchisee, you'll be treated with respect, not as a mere browser or "tire kicker."

That last point about being treated with respect brings up a good question: In general, how should you expect to be treated when visiting a franchisor? My answer is you should be treated professionally and as if your time is valuable. Beyond this answer, I have twofold advice:

1) Yes, you are also being evaluated by the franchise, but that doesn't mean they have the right to treat you like some sort of freshman fraternity pledge. If you are not happy with the levels of attention, information, or cooperation you are getting from a particular franchisor, it is probably not a good match for you (or, perhaps, for anybody).

2) The other side of this coin is you shouldn't become overly impressed by the attention that is likely to be lavished on you by the franchisor's staff. This is, after all, their job. Yes, you should be treated well, but you shouldn't allow such treatment to blind you to your real mission—finding out as much as possible about the franchisor and its franchisees. (As I have noted, inappropriate levels of fawning and attention may indicate an unhealthy eagerness on the part of the franchisor to get you to commit.)

The perception among potential franchisees is often one of, "I have money, I can buy what I want." But, of course, the actual situation is one where the franchisor has to want you as a franchisee before they'll want your money (unless, as I have said, they're unscrupulous or just don't care). You may have time, money, desire, and experience, but they still may or may not want you. Both parties have something to bring to the deal, so there has to be a mutually beneficial agreement. So, to bring about this possible "coming together" of interested parties, they will interview you as much as you interview them.

2) Obtaining and Analyzing Documents and Forms

A big part of visiting a franchisor is obtaining the necessary documents and forms, most notably the offering circular and the franchise agreement. The other major form is the franchisee application, sometimes euphemistically referred to as an "evaluation" or a "questionnaire." This is usually sent out to prospective franchisees ahead of time, but may be provided during the visit instead.

The offering circular provides vital and legally required information about the franchisor and its franchising program. The franchise agreement is a contract specifying the terms under which the franchisee and franchisor will do business together. This material can be a bit daunting, but it is required, and the information it presents will help you make the most educated final decision possible.

The other major form I mentioned above is the application, which you may have received before your visit. This form usually asks for detailed personal information about work history, finances, health, education, family, and various other categories. This can be an intimidating document (depending upon its tone), but, as is the case in most important personal and business dealings, the best way to fill it out is candidly and fully. You can be certain that unless this franchisor is bumbling and desperate for franchisees (and their cash!), the information you provide will be checked—so be certain that it is correct.

3) Talking to Current Franchisees

Hoover® Vacuum Cleaners used to use a motto that still concisely points out the value of the opinion of an experienced customer: "Ask the woman who owns one." Of course, even if that customer opinion is negative, it can be of just as much value, if not more, to the person considering the purchase. The same sort of horse's mouth information should be an essential part of evaluating a particular franchisor, but instead of asking a franchised chain's customers (i.e., those who buy its burgers, computers, or shoeshines), you need to ask the "consumers" who bought the franchise itself—you need to ascertain the opinions and experiences of a system's franchisees.

Start with information provided to you by the franchisor—a list of its franchisees, which may or may not be complete. Not every state requires that all franchisees be listed, but even if they are not all detailed, the total *number* of franchisees must be provided. So your first bit of analysis is to determine how forthright the franchisor has been in disclosing this information. Does it provide only as many franchisees as it has to list? Or is the franchisor more frank, perhaps even listing all of its franchisees? If a franchisor discloses only the minimum amount of franchisees they are required to give you, they may be trying to put a *happy face* on this part of their disclosure. This *partial* list may be only their system's *best* franchisees, in which case, you should do some independent research and come up with the names of a few franchisees who are not on the provided list. Calling these other franchisees, as well as those on the "approved" list, can help give a more balanced picture of being a franchisee of this prospective company.

Using this list, make some calls to a decent-size sampling of these franchisees. If at all possible, I suggest that you obtain a sample of at least twenty-five selected at random. It's a good idea to poll franchisees in various areas of the country, perhaps with a heavier concentration on franchisees in and around the area in which you are most interested in locating your outlet. Also, if such information is provided or can be obtained from current franchisees or another source, it can be illuminating to talk to one or more former franchisees, especially those who have recently left the system.

What should you say to these franchisees? You should be sure to fully identify yourself, telling them that you are considering becoming an XYZ franchisee, and that you would like to ask them a few questions about their franchise and their experiences with the franchisor. Do not be surprised if some do not wish to talk or want to take down your questions and get back to you (they may want to clear you and your questions through the franchisor, or they may just be very busy running their own businesses), but most will be used to such calls and should be happy to share information.

When you do start to ask them your questions, it best to begin with general, nonfinancial ones. Ask them things like: How long have you been an XYZ franchisee? Have you been satisfied with the support you received from the franchisor? What do you know now that you wish you knew when you first became a franchisee? What advice would you give someone considering becoming an XYZ franchisee? After getting answers to these sorts of questions, you can then move on to more specific inquiries. I strongly suggest you take written notes during this process—I have found that a short pencil is better than a long memory and a tape recorder beats a pencil.

You may want to preface your financial questions by telling the franchisee something to the effect that you realize financial information can be both a speculative and very personal thing, but you would appreciate getting their input on purchasing an XYZ as a purely financial endeavor. Try to make these questions broad and nonpersonal such as, "In your experience, what sort of annual rate of return on investment can an XYZ franchisee expect in their first few years in operation?" rather than, "How much money did you make in your first few years?"

Other questions to ask can include: How much money should an XYZ franchisee plan to have to pay for the total franchise investment? How much should an XYZ franchisee pay either himself or an employee to do the franchise's "main" job (whether that job is sales, supervision, or burger flipping)? What amount of money would you counsel an XYZ franchisee to have in reserve for "unexpected" expenses in the first year or two? Finally, you may be able to ask and get an answer to the $64,000 question, *How much did your franchise gross last year?*

To be sure, some franchisees may not want to tell you everything you want to know about these perhaps sensitive subjects. Even if they do answer all of your questions completely, you should not place 100 percent reliance on the responses. After all, as far as these franchisees know, you could be someone from their franchisor checking up on them, a spy for a competitor trying to gain an advantage, or even an IRS agent calling them! These are good reasons why even though you should make these sorts of calls, you should not place 100 percent reliance on the responses. All the more reason that more franchisors should provide potential franchisees with complete, candid, and clear earnings claims (see below).

4) Looking at Earnings Claims

First of all, I would like to say there are laws pertaining to the disclosure of potential earnings or revenues, but you should not believe any franchisor who tells you it's "against the law" or that he's "not allowed" to disclose such information. What is true is that it's against the law to disclose information on financial performance in any other way than that prescribed by the government, and of course, franchisors are not required to disclose this financial information. My research indicates some 80 percent do not do so. A growing number of franchisors, however, seem to be doing it more regularly, and I think even more should consider doing it. I believe full disclosure of earnings can only help both sides understand the entire situation more clearly.

In my opinion, it is unfortunate that the majority of franchisors do not provide these documents, which can be enlightening, informative, and useful. (Both to the franchisee and the franchisor. Nothing can help to sell franchises faster than being able to show they can make money!) Even when franchisors do provide earnings claims, they are often skewed by a desire to be precisely safe or to err on the side of conservatism. Some claims show only the performances of company-owned units or an "average" of all outlets in the system.

Some franchisors use earnings claims not to inform but to reduce their risk of a lawsuit by showing only stores that are not doing well. One major food franchisor used to issue an earnings claim that showed that every store that opened managed to lose $200,000. Now, you know that is not true—the company would have folded up their tents long ago if 100 percent of their franchisees were losing money. The reason for these very pessimistic figures was that if someone bought a franchise and did lose money, they would not be able to come after the franchisor saying that they had been misled about the financial risks. The franchisor could respond that the franchisee had been told up front that they would lose $200,000! A funny story, yes, but this example borders on abuse of what can (and should) be a valuable tool for both sides.

If a franchisor has elected not to prepare and present an earnings claim, should that make you suspicious? No. Remember that four out of five franchisors do not. It just means you will have to rely more heavily on your own research and estimates of the potential of the business. When provided, however, the information in an earnings claim can help in the next stage of your overall evaluation of a franchisor (or franchisors), looking at franchising as an investment.

What you should be suspicious about is if a franchisor gives you figures that are not in the offering circular. For instance, a salesperson might casually drop a remark to the effect that the last franchise he sold did $20,000 in sales just last week. If it is not in the legal documents, do not rely on it! So wonder to yourself, "Is he trying to put something over on me?"

After the Research

You have done plenty of research at this point, including visiting the franchisor, and you have been given the necessary documents. Perhaps you have even been told or will be told shortly that you are acceptable as a franchisee candidate. That's great! But there is a required ten business day waiting period after receiving the offering circular during which no money can change hands. During this period, you need to make another analysis (perhaps an even larger one than any of the others you have made) of the franchise you are considering buying. Before you commit to purchasing a particular franchise, you need to examine the transaction in terms of its impact as an investment.

Franchising as an Investment

Something I have observed over and over again in franchising is that too many people look at becoming a franchisee as simply "buying a job." In my opinion, not nearly enough potential franchisees look at it as an investment, too. Of course, buying a franchise is an investment of both time and money, and as with other investments, you should evaluate franchises based on the estimated return you can expect to get out of it.

Therefore, for those of you who are more financially oriented or, perhaps even more importantly, for those of you who are not financially savvy but who know that you should be or would like to be, here is a methodology of how prospective franchisees should look at this portion of the franchising equation. (Those of you who are totally unfamiliar with financial and cash-flow analysis would do well to read my bestseller, *How to Write a Winning Business Plan*, paying special attention to the material on pro formas.)

Becoming Educated Regarding Franchise Investments

Among the higher-priced investment franchises (such as hotels/motels, etc.), more often than not, the buyers are "high roller" types with financial advisors who help them closely examine the purely investment side of becoming a franchisee. In the lower price range (say $50,000 to $250,000), however, there is often a lack of knowledge and/or a lack of professional advisory services, which is why I am going to look at franchising now in strictly financial terms. I am going to treat your money as your slave, and put it to work for you.

The important yet simple point is that you should get as favorable and as competitive a rate of return as you possibly can for your franchise investment—but what should this rate be? Where do you find out what a reasonable rate of return is for your dollar? The first step is to look at what you can expect to make from comparable investments. For example, as this is being written, if you invest money in a ten-year Treasury note, you can expect to earn approximately 6 percent annually on your money; that 6 percent can be referred to as "the risk-free rate of return." If you take no risk with your money, you can earn 6 percent on it by doing nothing other than tying it up for a certain amount of time. Presumably, looking at it logically, you should therefore be able to earn something in excess of 6 percent by being willing to take more risk. Of course, there is no guarantee on the success of businesses, even franchised ones, and that's why I say you're taking a risk

Evaluating the Risk of a Franchise Investment

A principal tenet of investing says, "The higher the risk, the higher the return you should expect." Going back to the earlier risk continuum, the logical interpretation is that the greater the risk you're willing to take (by buying a newer franchise or a franchise in an unproven market) the greater the hoped-for return from that franchise should be, and, in general, how can you measure the risk of a franchising investment? The age and size of a franchisor is a good place to start. Usually, if a franchise system has been around for awhile and has multiple units, it has proven itself in a variety of markets, and *some* degree of risk has been taken out.

Other measures of risk are the answers to these two questions: (1) How many units has the franchisor sold recently? (2) How many of the franchisor's franchisees have failed recently? In the disclosure documents they furnish potential franchisees, franchisors are required to provide a list of: (1) People who own a franchise (often including the date the franchises were sold or opened) and (2) the number of franchisees that have been terminated or have gone out of business in the last three years. This information will help you answer the aforementioned questions.

First of all, has the franchisor sold many recent units? Unless it is a brand new franchisor, you should expect to see some recent sales. If there are not very many sales, is it because the franchisor is very discriminating when it comes to selecting franchisees? Or is it because, perhaps, potential franchisees have found the *franchisor* to be undesirable?

Next, check the number, and more importantly, the percentage of a franchisor's failed franchisees. Using the generally accepted 5 percent per-year closure rate of franchises as a general rule of thumb, determine if the franchisor's failure rate is higher or lower. If 10, 15, or even 20 percent of their franchisees have gone out of business in any recent year, something is wrong. Franchisees can be one of the greatest single factors in determining overall risk with that franchisor, whether it has five or five thousand franchises. Also, what are the percentages by year during the last few years? Is the proportion of failures falling or rising? If it's falling, perhaps the franchisor's "bad times" are ending and it is a good time to buy.

The bottom line is if the total number of failed franchisees exceeds five percent of a franchisor's total outlets, it means this franchisor has a higher failure rate than most other franchisors. This could be due to poor selection of franchisees, bad locations, incomplete training programs, tough competition, flawed expansion strategies, or incompetent management on the franchisor level. Or maybe the franchised business in question is a lemon! Whatever the reasons, you need to weigh the factors before you buy, not after.

When you purchase stock, you or your professional advisors look at its earnings and past performance and it should be no different when it comes to buying a franchise. Looking at the comparative failure rate of a franchisor's franchisees can be one of the greatest single factors in determining overall risk.

More Risk Equals More (Expected) Return

When trying to look more precisely at risk, particularly at the higher end of the risk scale, things are not quite as clear-cut as stated above. For example, you might find a franchise system that has higher-than-average failure rates, but whose general concept and business system you judge to be very solid. This might be a good, worthwhile risk, you deduce. You could then perhaps seek to buy out an established, but struggling, franchisee of this franchise, perhaps at much less than it would cost to buy a new outlet. If the only reasons the previous franchisee failed is that he or she lacked good individual management skills or was not using the right approach for his or her individual market, you might be able to make a much more successful go at it and realize a hefty return on your investment in the process. But, of course, there is risk involved. What if the reason the franchise was failing was the basic concept and system were not as solid as you thought? The risk lies in determining if a franchise in general or a specific unit is going to be successful. The higher the risk, the higher the estimated return you should expect to achieve before you decide to buy.

How Much Are You Worth to Yourself As an Employee?

Before you can determine your potential return on an investment in a franchise, you must consider an important concept that you may have overlooked or may not have properly assessed. Namely, you should be fairly compensated for the time you spend acting as a manager or "employee" of your franchised business on a day-to-day basis. However, before you start figuring just how generous you're going to be to yourself, you have to realize that the salary you should receive should only be *whatever the fair rate is for the job you're going to do* (such as managing a restaurant or changing a car's oil or whatever).

It does not matter that you might have been a top-flight sales-man or a CEO making six figures before you became a franchisee. You are a lube jockey or a fry cook now (in addition, of course, to being a franchisee and business owner). Your CEO or sales skills are not needed in that position, so you should not expect to make what you made before, not as a *salary*, anyway.

As an investment, you may well eventually make far more than you made before. And what should be a fair rate to pay yourself? The amount you would pay someone else to do the same job! Otherwise you're overpaying the employee (yourself) and underestimating the return to the investor (yourself).

Only after a fair salary for a manager is awarded to the owner (or whoever is going to do that job) can you calculate profit, and then return on investment.

Estimating Return

As I have said, there is more risk in investing in a franchise than in U.S. Treasury notes. On this higher risk end of the spectrum, you need to look for higher rates of return to make things worth your time and investment—but how high is higher?

Generally, you should look for at least one and a half to two times the risk-free rate of return on capital for most sorts of franchise invest-ments. That is to say that if you could get 8 percent risk-free (as I noted above), you should expect to get 12 percent to 16 percent, depending upon the risk involved (i.e., 16 percent for the riskiest, down to around 12 percent for less risky, but still not "blue chip" franchises). How much you can expect to make on a blue chip franchise, such as a McDonald's? About the middle of the range is a good expectation—the average return is about 13 to 14 percent. (Tales of McDonald's franchisees mak-ing 20 or 25 percent on what is a relatively riskless proposition are def-initely not unheard of, but do not weep in envy over these high figures. Either pay up the dough and get in the long line for a McDonald's fran-chise, or better yet, try and discover the *next* McDonald's, and get in on its ground floor.) All of these figures are standards to give you an idea of what to expect. As with any venture involving some amount of risk, the actual percentages may vary within these ranges. Or, of course, they may never materialize.

Remember that newer franchises may not have rosy histories of earnings or large numbers of outlets, but keep the general history of franchising in mind as you ponder these low (or nonexistent) numbers. For example, hamburger stands, video stores, and fast lube places all struggled at first until they became accepted and are now generally very successful and widespread franchised business. So if the concept seems strong and poised to succeed, you might wish to ignore anemic numbers, but you should expect to be compensated for this faith with a higher potential return for your investment.

Professional venture capital investment firms—of which there are several hundred in the United States—look to be compensated even *higher* than typical franchise rates when they make a decision to invest in a company. These professional financial risk takers regularly look for a return on investment from 35 percent to 70 percent annually, even up to *90 percent*. If you want a shot at these sorts of rates of return, we suggest you look at different business arenas than franchising. Instead, start your own business. Establish a copy of the video store or fast food outlet that you think is a winner, and if you're successful, all of the returns are yours. Keep in mind though, the high failure rate for independent businesses which most sources report. Yes, you may make more, but you're risking much more.

Comparing Initial Fees and Royalty Amounts

Two figures are important to understand when fully analyzing the financial end of owning a franchise: 1) the amount of the initial franchise fee, and 2) the percentage of the ongoing royalty, both of which are paid to the franchisor. Each figure has its significant points and possible misunderstandings.

1) Franchise Fees

The general rule of thumb for initial fees is: The greater the amount of the total initial investment, the lower the franchise fee should be as a percentage of the investment. This rule, such as it is, pertains only to single units, rather than multi-unit, area development, or subfranchise arrangements. The reason is franchisors do not want to create an impediment (through the imposition of gouging financial requirements) to people wanting to get into their business. For example, McDonald's charges a $225,000 franchise fee, and you might think, "They could charge whatever amount they want, even more than *ten times* that figure, and people would still line up to become a McDonald's franchisee." On the contrary, McDonald's would rather see their franchisees have plenty of money in reserve to run the business or to maybe even open another outlet.

At the other end of the spectrum are service-type franchises, such as cleaning services or professional consultants. Their fees may be half or more of the total investment. The reason? These are generally *not* capital-intensive businesses. Franchisees usually do not have to buy land or buildings or extensive in-plant equipment, and therefore the fee is much higher in comparison to the other costs. Does this mean that these fees are high simply because that's what the franchisor feels it can charge? Usually not, because in these cases what you're paying for, usually at a fraction of a price it would cost to develop them yourself, are the systems, technology, and materials the franchisor has developed, plus, if appropriate, the advantages of cooperative buying and advertising.

In short, you should try to determine if the initial fee seems fair, but you should not put overriding importance on this figure. By itself, neither the franchise fee nor the royalty percentage (covered below) should be a factor influencing whether or not someone becomes a franchisee of a particular franchisor. Instead, you must look at the entire investment and what you can expect in return.

Prospective franchisees need to get over the barrier they often have in their minds that they are paying a fee of say, $50,000, just to "join the club"—a sort of initiation fee. Franchisees are not joining a "club" or simply paying for the rights to a business's name (at least, they should not be merely paying for a name—I have shown earlier all the components that a franchisee should expect in return for their investment).

You should also realize the franchise fee is the only source of initial income to the franchisor while they train you and set you up. You may be paying $500,000 or more for your franchise (excluding the fee), but that amount does not go to the franchisor. Instead, it purchases land and buildings, equipment, inventory, and so forth.

2) The Ongoing Royalty Percentage

If, as I have shown you, franchisees are not paying a capricious initiation fee to franchisors, neither are they paying a permanent percentage of their income to the franchisor just for being allowed to operate. Again, that royalty pays for support, advice, research and development, and, above all else, a proven business system and the expertise to successfully operate it. Look at the situation this way: Would you rather pay nothing to anyone but have a much higher chance of losing your investment? Or would you be willing to pay perhaps 8 percent in royalties for an established concept and earn maybe 15 to 20 percent on your capital?

Once the general overall benefits of the royalty have been determined, next you have to look at the specific figure and what you can expect to get for it. It is important not to judge a royalty simply by its gross amount—that is, do not look at the situation as follows: The XYZ Company charges 8 percent, but the ABC Company only charges 6 percent. You have to examine it in terms of what it will cost you in real dollars and what it gets you as an investor. In other words, 8 percent *of what* and *for what*, compared to 6 percent *of what* and *for what*? What are the franchise's sales likely to be? What services will the amount buy you?

For example, in the case of McDonald's, between royalty and rent (because they typically own the land on which their franchises are located), they charge their franchisees approximately 12 percent of total gross sales, but the annual return on investment these franchises realize can be from 13 and up! On the other hand, if John's Burgers charges only a 4 percent royalty and returns maybe 8 percent on your investment, you're not being logical if you go with John's only because 4 is less than 12. (Obviously, this oversimplifies things a bit, but you get the point). Do not get lulled into thinking that low royalty amounts will save you money. Low royalties generally translate into a low level of service and a low return. Of course, if all other things are equal (such as total investment, national or regional reputation, level of service, and rate of return), but a certain franchisor's rate is lower, you should probably go with the lower rate.

You have to expect that the franchisor should realize a financial return for establishing you in business and for providing you with their proven expertise, and, as I have shown, the initial fee sure does not cover those things with much of a profit margin. So do not look at a royalty as a negative, and do not begrudge the franchisor that money. It is merely part of the cost of doing business as a franchisee.

Now that you have a better idea of what franchising can do for your money, how do you get the money to accomplish all of this?

Financing Options

Of course, you have likely been thinking about this all along. How am I going to pay for this? I am going to touch on only a few points here; entire books have been written about financing franchises or other small businesses.

In general, since methods of financing can vary greatly from person to person and from situation to situation, I can only offer some advice, some facts, and a little direction. The first and perhaps most important rule of financing a franchise is not to underestimate the amount of money you will need. It's only natural to try to be frugal and optimistic when planning how much money you'll need (or, more likely, how much debt you will have to take on), but my rule of thumb is to figure out how much you *think* you will need, and then add 10 to 20 percent. Remember what I said about undercapitalization often ruining franchises!

The bottom line is that most franchisees put down between 20 to 40 percent of the total cost and finance the rest. Where does this financed money come from? The figures I gathered from the franchisors who responded to the Francorp/DePaul University survey can provide a partial answer. According to this study, while 41 percent of the respondents provided some kind of financing to their franchisees, a substantial number of other franchisors offered no direct financing, but instead recommended franchisees to lenders who were likely to be responsive to the franchisees' needs. Other interesting figures gleaned from the responses of these franchisors: 20 to 28 percent of their franchisees receive at least some amount of Small Business Administration (SBA) financing; around half of their franchisees tap into the equity in their home; and up to 75 percent of their franchisees pledged personal assets as collateral to obtain a bank loan.

Seven Sources to Look for Franchise Financing

1) **Personal Wealth.** Your home(s), car(s), savings, art, jewelry, and other valuables can be used to finance your franchise, but, as I have pointed out, it's best not to go in with your "last dime" in case some level of financial reserves is needed.

2) **"F & F" Financing.** F & F stands for family and friends. The advantage of borrowing from these sources (or selling them equity in your franchise) is they know you and presumably like you. The disadvantage is if things go badly, they may like you less later. According to the Francorp/DePaul survey, some 22 percent of franchisees utilize this source of financing.

3) **The Franchisor.** The above-cited 41 percent figure is encouraging, and it's 10 percent higher than the figure for this question in a previous survey conducted by the same organizations, showing that more franchisors are offering at least some form of financing to their franchisees.

4) **Banks.** In general, straight bank financing has become harder to get for franchisees, but there are financial institutions that do lend to franchisees. A little research can help boost your chances (especially if that research includes a reference from your franchisor).

5) **Leasing.** This can be a way to obtain equipment, fixtures, and even the business's location. Many franchisors also have preexisting arrangements with suppliers to assist their new franchisees. The cost of leasing can be high, but it can also reduce your overall debt.

6) **Government Sources.** There is usually a considerable amount of "red tape" wrapped around these sources of money, such as SBA or equivalent state-agency loans, but they can be worth investigating. See the SBA chapter in this book for more help.

7) **Venture Capital and/or Limited Partnerships.** This solution is usually confined to very large investments, such as an entire franchising territory. In return, you will likely have to give up a big chunk of equity, but most franchisors require you to retain more than 50 percent of the franchise ownership.

After securing financing, the final immediate step before the close is the mostly precautionary process of having your legal and accounting professionals review the contracts and figures, a step I call "bringing in the pros."

Bringing in the Pros

At this stage, you should have your personal attorney (or business attorney, if you have one) look over the offering circular and, especially, the franchise agreement. However, I make that suggestion with the following caveat: The material points included in these documents are almost universally *not* negotiable. Your attorney will not be involved in drafting these documents or negotiating compromises on their component points, but will rather provide you with guidance and advice. The same holds true for your accountant, if you wish to use one to go over the numbers involved (this is always a good idea). This advice can be valuable, but by now you should know far more about the franchisor than any advisor could glean by a quick look at these documents, so be sure to weigh any objections against what you already know (and feel). However, if these professional advisors strenuously object to points or terms that the franchisor cannot clearly and respectfully justify to your satisfaction, perhaps you should not go with this particular franchisor.

One final point on professional advisors: Be sure to agree on the "scope of engagement" in advance. That is, make it clear what you want them to do and what you do not want, and get a good idea of the cost involved. For example, you do not want your attorney to start rewriting parts of the franchise agreement. You just want her to tell you if she sees serious problems with any of its provisions.

The Longest Two Weeks You Will Ever Spend

Suppose that, upon meeting with a franchisor, you decide to buy the franchise. The ten-business day waiting period before you can actually sign the agreement can go one of two ways—either it will pass relatively quickly, with very little apprehension, because you feel good and secure about a decision to buy, or it can drag, with doubts growing each day until you're not sure if you want to go through with the whole thing. If the latter is the case, maybe you *do not* want to go through with it. When push comes to shove, maybe franchising just *is not* right for you, no matter your test score. If this is true, it's better to find out now (even considering the amount you may have spent to discover it) than to feel trapped into committing even more time and money to what will likely be a failure or (at best) an unenjoyable undertaking.

Just because you feel nervous does not necessarily mean that you have made the wrong decision. At least some amount of "buyer's remorse" is normal with a purchase or investment of this magnitude. If you do feel overly anxious about the decision, review the reasons why you thought it was a good decision. Talk to the franchisor's representative (you'll likely hear from him or her anyway during this period!) and ask specific questions about things you may feel nervous or unclear about. But most of all, look within yourself and ask, "Is this the right thing for me to do now?" After all the mental hemming and hawing that is likely to accompany this question, if the answer is still yes, get your checkbook ready and move on to the next (and final!) step in this long process.

The Close

If everything is as it should be—from your desire to be in (and your aptitude for) the franchisor's line of business to complete and properly drafted paperwork—the next step is simply to execute the aforementioned documents, write a check to the franchisor, and shake hands.

But first...

When it comes time to sign the check and make the ultimate decisions, your emotions will likely come into play. Do you feel comfortable with everything? This *definitely* is the time to ask any questions, *not* after you have signed on and paid up. Of course, you'll have many questions then, but right now we're referring to basic, fundamental questions that should affect your overall decision.

And then, after any last-minute questions have been answered, you are ready. Your hand may be a bit unsteady, but remember this: With all the advice you have received and all the research you did, your decision should be pretty steady by now. So sign on the dotted line, and get ready for the adventure you have been looking forward to. You are now a franchisee!

Chapter 7

How to Persuade Like an Entrepeneur

Persuasion is a blend of three old skills: selling, motivating, and negotiating. You have to be excellent at it if you run your own business. Being good at it is not enough.

Entrepreneurs are rainmakers. They make rain happen, and to do it often, they fake it before they make it. Sometimes they cross the line and are labeled cons or crooks. Entrepreneurs often play by the rules when they win, but they change the rules when they lose so they can win.

Again, I do not condone or encourage their behavior, but I find that most rainmakers at certain times are indistinguishable from a "con."

Entrepreneurial Con Artists?

You don't have to be crazy to be an entrepreneur, but it could help. In an article in *The Journal of Creative Behavior*, management professors Erik K. Winslow and George T. Solomon of George Washington University say the psychological profile of successful entrepreneurs resembles in certain ways that of criminally insane "sociopaths" who commit crimes while feeling little or no remorse.

Both entrepreneurs and sociopaths are typically "charming, spontaneous, and likeable on first meetings and ambivalent about close personal relationships. Both are opportunistic and are uncomfortable with rules, conventional wisdom, and others' expectations."

In its core assumptions, the entrepreneur culture that arose in the 1980s resembles the anticonventional hippie culture of the 1960s. The authors say entrepreneurs need detachment to withstand setbacks.

Their psychic opposite is the risk-averse manager.

MANAGER (Conventional)	ENTREPRENEUR (Mildly Sociopathic)
Very conscious of taboos and rules.	Views rules as guidelines only.
Sensitive to the future and adept at postponing gratification.	Concept of the future is based on his own fantasy of it.
Has a powerful need for acceptance.	Ambivalent toward control, success, responsibility.
Able to identify the problems in any course of action.	Can be manipulative and exploitative in personal relationships.
Makes detailed plans.	Impatient with discussion, theories. Seems impulsive. Prone to action.

One person in history seems to have successfully straddled both camps: the legendary Phineas Taylor Barnum, one of the founders of the Barnum and Bailey Circus. His other legacy is the saying, "There's a sucker born every minute." This statement has stood the test of time.

If you think the modern day con will not be viewed by history as a Robin Hood, odds are you are naive. If you're ever in Bridgeport, Connecticut, go to 820 Main Street to a three-story Victorian brownstone museum. Can you guess who was mayor of this southern Connecticut town from 1875-76, and who is the hero of this museum? I'll give you a hint—he also gave the world "the greatest show on earth." Yes, we have a serious museum dedicated to P.T. Barnum, and it draws crowds every day. Once when I visited with my family, I thought I saw P.T. outside scalping theater tickets, but it might have been done with mirrors. You never can be sure, and that's why a sucker is born every minute.

In his day, P.T. was a rainmaker. Con men and rainmakers both use those principles, but as Professor Karel Vesper, a leading academic in entrepreneurship from the University of Seattle in Washington, says, only one uses them to create real value.

So cons and entrepreneurs should be judged by the eyes of the sucker—enough said. Following are three basic traits of human behavior that everyone who persuades uses, whether "con" or not:

1) The Pygmalion Effect
2) The Jelly Bean Principle
3) The Length of Pieces of String

The Pygmalion Effect

When it comes to hiring help, there are two schools of thought. The first says, "Let's automate everything and hire unskilled, low-paid people for everything else." Many entrepreneurs go this route in the early stages of company development, figuring that it will keep costs down, but before long they see that they can't get quality work.

The second school of thought starts out with good people and pays them good salaries from the beginning. I agree with that approach.

I have concluded that you don't motivate employees—they motivate themselves. As a manager, your job is not to demotivate them. Rainmakers select only motivated employees as the single best method of improving their firms' performance.

A fascinating piece of behavioral research, conducted by two Harvard doctoral candidates in the field of education, is called the Pygmalion, or "late bloomer" effect. Here's how it was conducted: All the fourth grade pupils in the San Francisco public schools were asked to take an I.Q. test. The researchers then sent a personal letter to a random selection of fourth grade teachers. The letter was short, personal, and to the point. In essence, it said:

"Johnny Jones, who is in your class, is probably not performing at his full potential, according to our testing. We see strong signs that Johnny may be a genius but that he also appears to be a late bloomer.

We judged it best to alert you to this finding, but we suggest you don't share the information with anyone until a future determination can be conducted."

Each letter was typed and personally signed.

One year later, the students who were fictitiously labeled late bloomers were tested again, and their performance was analyzed against the performance of the group as a whole. I don't really need to tell you the results, do I? The study wouldn't be worth relating to you unless the change was significant, and it was!

The message here that of the self-fulfilling prophecy. When someone young enough to develop is given small signs of encouragement, great developments can occur. The power of words of encouragement toward your younger employees can be staggering. You can actually improve their performance simply by raising your expectations about their possibilities. If you think they are good and communicate this to them, they just might become good.

Here's another entrepreneurial persuasion technique called the placebo effect. Most of us are aware of this phenomenon. People who are told a drug will have a certain effect will many times experience that effect, even when given an empty pill with no active properties. Norman Cousins, who learned firsthand the power of belief in eliminating his own illness, concludes, "Drugs are not always necessary. Belief in recovery always is."

The Jelly Bean Principle

The jelly bean principle explains why entrepreneurs and financiers seldom see events in the same perspective. I came up with this principle when I decided to run a little experiment during one of my seminars for entrepreneurs and bankers.

During lunch, I brought out a big glass jar filled with red jelly beans. I placed it next to the podium on a little table. I then pointed out the window to a black Mercedes parked on the street below and announced that the car would be awarded to the person who could guess *exactly* how many jelly beans were in the jar. The person whose guess was merely closest would *not* receive a prize.

I did this in both the entrepreneurs' and the bankers' seminars. Each person was given one guess, which they wrote on a piece of paper. Both entrepreneurs and bankers took about the same amount of time to guess. They all eyed the jelly bean jar, picked it up, and felt its weight. The distribution of guesses in both groups was a bell-shaped curve, with 1,000 as the mean. For both groups, the guesses looked roughly like this: 1,101; 886; 1,161; 1,211; 547; 1,762; 671; 981; 662; 666; 1,865; 786; 630; 455; 1,331; 1,470; 1,541; 1,030.

After the initial guesses were all written on the blackboard, I moaned it was such a shame not to be able to give away that wonderful car. (I sometimes struggled with the ethical question of what I would do if someone actually guessed correctly: Would I eat one jelly bean or give away a stranger's car? Is that a con?) I enthusiastically announced a second round of guesses, with the car going to the person who came closest. This got everyone's attention.

In the first round, both the bankers and the entrepreneurs made guesses that formed a bell-shaped curve. In the second round, though, things changed dramatically. The bankers' curve narrowed until it formed an almost straight vertical line around the mean, which was 1,000. The entrepreneurs' curve, on the other hand, spread out horizontally until it was almost flat. In the second round, the bankers bunched up their guesses around the mean of the original distribution. Because there was no hard data to work with, they chose to create data, and they bunched (like turkeys and sheep) their answers around an imputed norm, where it was safe and warm. The entrepreneurs made second guesses that ranged from 300 to 3,000. They all grabbed for their own share of turf, figuring that way they'd have a better chance of being the closest to the unknown figure. The natural tension between bankers and entrepreneurs comes from the fact they are different psychological types. Entrepreneurs are driven by nature to strike out on their own, away from the pack, while bankers are driven to play it safe and minimize their losses. Each is in a different business because each is a different kind of person.

The Length of Pieces of String

Another experiment I did for bankers involved eight pieces of string. Seven pieces were 22 inches long, but the eighth piece was only 18 inches long. The strings were laid out on a table with one end of each aligned to the others so that everyone could clearly see that all the strings except the last one were the same length.

I then planted six stooges in the room. Actually they were entrepreneurs, but I made them wear nice three-piece suits so they looked like bankers. The stooges were instructed to say that the strings were all the same length. Then I brought in the subject, usually a financial type. After a few warm up questions, I asked the subject if the strings on the table were the same length. While he was thinking, I asked each stooge the same question. So what do you think this poor banker said after hearing his "peers" agreed that the strings were the same length? Naturally, he concurred.

No matter how I did it, the results of the experiment were always the same. I tried it on a bunch of different bankers at the seminar and tried varying the number of stooges from two to eight. It didn't matter. When a banker heard more than one other person who he thought was a banker say the strings were the same length, he agreed.

The findings were fascinating, but the experiment was getting a little boring, so I devised a variation, sort of a "con" on a con. I told one of the stooges to say that he thought the eighth string was shorter. What do you know? Our banker suddenly became a hero, now that he had an ally! He said, "Hey, there's a short piece of string there!"

I concluded that it's almost impossible to persuade someone of something that is not true if that person has one or more trusted allies for the truth.

This string experiment tells a great deal about human behavior, and its applications are intuitively obvious to a great persuader. If one of a tribe's high-ranking braves loses faith in the rainmaker's dance, the chances of rain are greatly diminished. Smoke screens and mirages will only delay the downfall of the rainmaker because the die is cast when the heads of the hunting parties no longer believe.

As you have undoubtedly observed, I believe there is a little "con" in every persuader. To accomplish so much, to be a high achiever, often requires a persuader who creates double images or even mirages. They always use smoke screens. Persuaders often straddle the line between right and wrong in an all-out effort to make others see their vision.

But persuasion is not stealing and persuasion is not lying, and entrepreneurial persuaders don't do either. A good card player doesn't need to cheat.

Cheating, lying, and stealing are not fun, and they spoil the game. Yet, in most persuasion activities, where and how wide to draw the line is an individual choice. It involves creating mirages and smoke screens rather than lying or cheating. It's more challenging to create a mirage.

The Seven-Step Selling Process

Of the three great skills which make up persuasion—negotiating, motivating, and selling—the greatest of these three is selling. It alone can fix all the problems in growing a small business. I have never encountered a problem in business which can not be solved by selling more—a lot more. Here is some specific help to allow you to sell more.

What is the key ingredient to starting a business? No, it's not money or enthusiasm, or a good idea. It's a customer. It's the only ingredient that is both sufficient and necessary. When someone finally says, "I'll buy that," a business begins.

How do you get to that ultimate point? How do you turn your prospects into buyers? No subject in the field of management has been analyzed more with less impact than selling. Because of this, many models have sprung up. The one I like best is the seven-step selling process. I call it the entrepreneurial persuasion model.

Step 1 - Research (Buy From vs. Sell To)
Step 2 - Prospecting
Step 3 - Approach and Preheat
Step 4 - Qualifying the Buyer
Step 5 - Presenting the Product
Step 6 - Handling Objections—Feel, Felt, Found
Step 7 - Gaining Commitment

Step 1: Research (Buy From vs. Sell To)

Nobody likes to be sold to. What Fred Smith of Federal Express did while raising money to start an industry was allow someone to participate in an opportunity. He did not sell to, he allowed the customer the privilege of buying from. In hindsight, I wish he had given me a chance to get a little of that early Federal Express stock—how about you?

Keep in mind this principle: Whenever you are *selling to* somebody, that person is going to resist you. If you hold open your hand and push outward on another person's hand, the natural reaction is to push back. Pressure generates resistance.

Buying from is just the opposite. It generates assistance, not resistance. It generates opportunities and friendships. It's when two hands are joined and a handshake results.

Research takes the cold out of sales calls. It is the key to the entrepreneurial persuasion selling model. Research occurs at the beginning of the selling process and lays the foundation for what follows. When the foundation is weak, the building is suspect.

During the research phase, you need to discover the answers to the other six steps before they occur. When you skip the research, you have to hope that your "preheat" or your ability to handle objections will do the job. Hope is a poor substitute for research.

During research you need to answer the same questions sought after by all good journalists: Who, what, why, when, and where? Here are a few questions that you need to answer in the selling process:

When?
When to install?
When to implant?
When to monitor?
When to influence?
When to call?
When to make an appointment?
When to close?
When to service?
When to deliver?
When to bill?
When to get referrals?
When to get testimonials?

What?
What is their business?
What is their need?
What is their situation?
What is their hot button?
What is their financial ability?

Where?
Where is the competition?
Where are their markets?
Where are they going?
Where have they been?
Where is their niche?
Where is their expertise?
Where is the hidden opportunity?

Who?	Why?
Receptionist	Why are they confused?
Executive Secretary	Why are they unsure?
Administrative Assistant	Why are they in a hurry?
Decision Maker	Why are they buying?
Team	Why are they using the competition?
Current Supplier	

Step 2: Prospecting

"The hours we pass with happy prospects in view are more pleasing than those crowned with fruition."

—Oliver Goldsmith, *The Hermit,* 1764

For many products, prospecting or determining the most logical location for customers is the hardest part of the selling process. Once you find the right person, the product's benefits can gain the customer's interest. Prospecting is plain hard work, and there are no known shortcuts or easy methods to do it! This is especially true for intangible products (insurance, stocks and bonds, or any services).

Step 3: Approach and Preheat

During the approach, two major actions should occur. First, a salesperson should reduce relationship tension. In other words, you and the customers should feel at ease. Selling is not you doing something to the customer, but a shared experience in which you solve the customer's problem together. At the same time, the salesperson should build task tension by showing concern for the customer's needs, such as, "I understand that you don't have a dishwasher. I understand that you need a new car. I understand…" The task that needs to be accomplished creates task tension. Selling is not a totally social exchange. You are there to represent your products and services. The other person is there for the service or the product you offer.

Preheating during the approach can also help take the cold out of sales calls. This step includes awards, testimonials, articles, and, most important of all, referrals—all designed to warm the client to your approach. Allow your current and past customers to brag for you. Preheat is not a computerized form letter. That's called direct mail.

Preheating lets your customers help you sell other customers. When your approach begins with a referral, you are on your way to success.

As you approach your prospects, keep in mind that most decisions to do business are made during the first five minutes. Don't underestimate the power of an early bias for or against you. You never get a second chance to make a first impression.

Step 4: Qualifying the Buyer

This is the "hot button," and it focuses on the reason the buyer will eventually buy. Every product or service hits several salient features and attributes. Some of them are more important to certain customers than others. Not everyone buys the same product for the same reason. The objective of Step 4 is to determine what turns the specific customer on. What button do you push to get the order? What does the customer need? This can be gained only through a careful questioning of the customer. During Step 4, you must probe, discover, and question (PDQ) to determine the dominant buying motive (DBM). I like to call it the hot button.

Step 5: Presenting the Product

Within this sales model, most sales personnel do this step best. They are so familiar with their product, having presented it numerous times, that they can usually make a convincing presentation about its features and benefits. The only issue here is to stress the benefits the customer receives from the product, which are the perceived values, versus its features, which explain how your product is made or functions. Because most salespeople do this so well, I won't dwell on it.

Step 6: Handling Objections—Feel, Felt, Found

After the product has been presented, there will undoubtedly be some objections, attempts to postpone purchase, or discussion of the weaknesses of your product. How do you handle these objections? The key is to avoid conflict to frame things so that a person is doing what he or she wants to do, not what you want. It's very hard to overcome resistance. It's much easier to avoid it by building on agreement. I call this the "feel, felt, found" approach, and here's how it works:

1) Listen. Don't interrupt; get the full objection before you respond.
2) Cushion or acknowledge it. Objections are usually not foolish, so empathize with the person and try to legitimize his or her feelings. Acknowledge that others have had similar objections. In fact, you can say that you understand how they feel and that others have felt that way, too.
3) Question. Remember, asking is the key to persuading. To handle an objection, you must unearth its source. Only then can you explain it away.
4) Answer. The first three parts focus on validating and understanding objections. Part 4 focuses on turning the negative aspects into positive answers. This is done by introducing new information. You might say something like, "You are really only partially informed. We have found some new evidence that will put your mind to rest about our products." Customers are never wrong, but sometimes they are only partially informed. It's your job to supply the missing, pivotal information. The object is to spin the objection around and to use the power of the problem to be the power behind your persuasive answer.
5) Confirm. Be sure to confirm that what you said is what was heard. Ask prospects to repeat what was just said to be sure they got it. It helps to program what you just said into their brain. When they repeat, they begin to accept what you have said. "Do you see any good business reason why we shouldn't start today?" It is a confirmation of an objection that has been spun around and is now the reason to buy. Don't give them a chance, just a choice. "Can we do business now, or do I need to tell you more about it?" is another way to confirm.

The secret to your success is in how you handle those objections. Answer each question carefully. The goal is to reduce the risk to zero. To do this you need to learn to take an objection and turn it around so that it works for you instead of against you.

Step 7: Gaining Commitment

This has traditionally been classified as the most important sales step, but it is not. Actually, the most vital sales step is qualifying the buyer (Step 3). If that is completed properly and the approach is done properly, gaining commitment is the smallest and least stressful step in the entire selling process. To gain commitment, you may want to create an opportunity to close on an objection. Many objections can be handled by exercising the feel, felt, found technique. It is called a "trial close."

Sometimes salespeople enjoy the selling process so much that they go past the close and keep presenting the product rather than stop to make the sale. For instance, suppose a customer is buying a house and likes everything about it but the location. You can't do anything about that, so you are not going to make the sale, and you must realize that. If, on the other hand, the objection occurs because the house has no fireplace and the customer continues to hang on that issue, don't make the mistake of saying, "You don't need a fireplace in today's society; a fireplace takes up the heat," or "it's a poor energy choice," or whatever.

Rather, you should acknowledge whatever the customer really wants. If a fireplace is important, accept the conclusion. The way to close on an objection is to say, "Do you like the location? Do you like the house? Is the price okay?" If the answer is yes, you can say, "You mean you would buy this house if it had a fireplace?" If the customer says yes, you only have to negotiate the price of the fireplace, and you have gained commitment.

Selling is the art of reaching agreement and building trust. The professional salesperson is an artist with a keen set of listening skills and an inner desire to perform. The whole world is your customer, and you're selling every day to everyone, so why not get good at it?

Models like the one outlined in this chapter are useful to a degree, but they are only models. A practicing salesperson also needs to know some basic principles of persuasion that are grounded in experience. Following are several such principles.

Pareto's 80/20 Philosophy

No concept in selling is more powerful than the Pareto Principle. It is wonderfully simple, and, in my view, it is more useful and accurate than systems that classify buyers and sellers into different types. Although it was discovered during the ancient civilizations in Rome and Greece, the 80/20 rule was popularized in the eighteenth century by the Italian philosopher, Pareto. It means that 80 percent of sales are made by 20 percent of the people. To view the principle from a buyer's point of view, consider that 80 percent of all products bought are purchased by 20 percent of the buyers.

And you may also think of 80/20 as a reminder that 80 percent of the successes you enjoy come from 20 percent of your activities, or that 80 percent of all problems in a company are caused by 20 percent of the employees. Feel free to add to this formula. But whatever you do to make it meaningful to you, write out the details of your 80/20 descriptions.

The point of all this is to remind you that few people are usually responsible for most of what happens. If it is true that 80 percent of all business is done by 20 percent of all the people, it is very important that you not waste your time with the 80 percent who do only 20 percent of the business! When you combine two or more of these Pareto principles, you can really begin to focus your efforts.

Believability, Likability, and Trust

A second idea that has stood the test of time is the concept of believability, likability, and trust (BLT). It too is simple: People buy only from other people who have BLT. Persuasion is the art of building trust and confidence. Trust is built by doing what you say you will do. It's not complicated; it's just hard to do.

Combine BLT with Pareto's 80/20, and you have a useful formula for selling:

1) Be agreeable. Always smile and be happy.
2) Give others the attention they need. Hold the spotlight on them, not you.
3) Make others feel admired. Talk about them, not about YOU.

4) Make others feel appreciated. Don't forget to say "Thank you"

5) Make others feel accepted. Never put someone down.

6) Make others feel approved. He who judges is judged.

7) Give others cooperation and help. This creates friendship instead of resistance.

8) Make others feel important. Help them accomplish their goals, not yours.

9) Make others feel needed. Be vulnerable and allow them to help you.

10) Make others feel you trust them. It's a two-way street.

11) Bonus method: Don't be ashamed to say, "If you'll give me 5 percent of your trust to start, I'll earn the remaining 95 percent."

The Difference between Marketing and Selling

The difference between a marketing versus sales orientation can be determined partially by how you handle the subtle difference between a product's features and its corresponding customer benefits. Marketing is a customer looking for a product, whereas selling is a product looking for a customer. It's the same transaction, but it's either going forward or backward (see the figure below).

An example of this distinction is highlighted in the quarter-inch drill story. An estimated 3,250,000 quarter-inch drills were sold in this country last year, which means that customers bought 3,250,000 holes that year. It just happened that the drill was necessary to produce the hole. If anyone is ever able to package a hole, customers would begin buying the holes to solve their problem.

Charles Revson, the entrepreneur founder of Revlon, the famous cosmetics company, once expressed the same thing in another way. He said, "In my factory we make cosmetics, but in my stores we sell hope." Customers buy benefits, while you make features. A customer benefit is a product feature turned inside out.

Finding a Market Niche

Think small—that's the advice I've often given to entrepreneurs. By finding a slice of the market that's been ignored because it seems too small, you can often turn out a profitable niche for yourself with minimum marketing effort and expense. Persuaders like niches better because they are often less competitive.

Defining the market is crucial. I can't tell you how often I've heard that potential market for someone's product or idea was "every man, woman, and child." The funny thing is, I've never seen one of these products make it to market. This kind of thinking means that the market hasn't been defined. It's better to find an existing need and fill it than to work in an undefined market.

Tom Drewes, president of Quality Books in Lake Bluff, Illinois, has done just that. His company distributes books by small publishers to the library market. "Libraries are a $2 billion market," he says, "and most of that market is covered by the large wholesalers and the publishers themselves." Drewes estimates that as little as 1/10 of 1 percent of sales to libraries are small press books. That's a mighty small niche, but it's worth millions a year to his company.

Price alone isn't a niche. If all you offer is a cheap price, then someone else is going to come along and knock you off. Consider the personal computer market. A quick glance at any computer magazine will show you that there are dozens of mail-order companies selling no-name IBM PC clones at rockbottom prices. Twenty small companies competing for the low end of the market hardly qualify as a niche. However, mail order companies like Dell Corporation have created a niche as they eliminate or reduce margins for retailers.

Once you've got a niche, service the hell out of it. When you've got a good niche, you'll get business just by being there. If you don't do a good job, your customers might look elsewhere, but if you service it well, you might find yourself with a permanent niche.

Here's Drewes's approach: "We listen to our customers. We sell millions of books one at a time. That requires patience and hard work, and maybe that's why no one else has come into the market to compete with us directly." That keeps the niche attractive.

The Product Life Cycle

Be aware of your product's life cycle. The life of a product or a service has four phases: (1) start-up, (2) growth, (3) maturity, and (4) decline. At the start-up phase, the market hasn't yet developed, so the chance of finding a viable niche is limited. In the growth stage, the market is blossoming with niches. When the market reaches the mature stage, the niches tend to diminish. But niches sometimes reappear when a product's life cycle begins its decline. In fact, they occur whenever significant change occurs in the market structure. When the slope of the life cycle curve changes rapidly, that change creates niches.

Don't get too comfortable. A successful niche doesn't last forever. Markets change as do customers' needs and attitudes. Keep your eye on your own market and on other markets for opportunities, and be prepared to make changes if you see the market beginning to dwindle. One percent of a thriving market can be very profitable, while five percent of a fading market can leave you awash in red ink.

Market Strategy—Think Small

Developing a marketing strategy is one of the more elusive procedures within the marketing discipline, especially for smaller, less well-heeled companies. A clever strategy, to "think small," was what David needed to defeat Goliath. A simplified example serves the point better than a statement of what it means.

In the early 1970s, the ten major soap manufacturers were investigating the market for a soap concentrate for home washing machines. They reasoned that the large-size boxes of laundry detergents could be reduced to the size of an aspirin bottle while still retaining the necessary cleaning power. A concentrate would have the advantage of reducing the manufacturing plant, warehousing, shipping costs, supermarket retail space, and storage space in the laundry room. So an idea for a soap pill was conceived and one entry was a product known as Salvo (Procter & Gamble).

During the marketing research, each of the ten soap manufacturers conducted independent studies to determine the characteristics that the soap pill should possess. An element of the research was the suds capacity of the new concentrate. In other words, should it be a high sudser or a low sudser?

On the one hand, the high sudser had the advantage of appearing to be really cleaning. It had the disadvantage of upsetting those concerned about polluting the rivers and lakes, or even their own septic systems. The other alternative, the low sudser, had very few pollution disadvantages, but if you looked into your washing machine, you might wonder if the pill was really cleaning. It was a fundamental question about the ideal product characteristics, and the research, conducted independently by all ten manufacturers, concluded that 80 percent of the housewives wanted a high-sudsing tablet for its visual cleaning assurances.

Nine of ten manufacturers interpreted the data and produced the high-suds product. They began to fight over that 80 percent share of the market, each eventually settling for an average of about 9 percent market share. Meanwhile, the tenth company, a clever little marketing-oriented firm, produced a good nonpolluting low sudser and captured 20 percent of the market.

Everyone operates from the same basic marketing facts, but when establishing marketing strategies, it is a good idea to "think small" in small businesses. If you are clever enough to pick a good niche, you might not need persuasive skills. "Being a big fish in a small pond" is another way of saying "market niching."

The Dogs Won't Eat the Dog Food: The Importance of Product

In sales folklore, there is no more popular story than the one called by its punch line, "The dogs won't eat the dog food." In fact, I tried to trace its origins and found it impossible to pinpoint when it started. It has passed from generation to generation, reappearing in many dialects in numerous sales situations. I first heard the story more than 25 years ago when I served at the feet of marketing guru Ted Levitt. It goes something like this:

At a large national meeting of the marketing department and sales force of a major dog food manufacturer, the marketing manager and promotion manager are delivering long-winded speeches about new strategies designed to increase their market share. Unfortunately, the results of every marketing brainstorm developed at previous sales meetings have been disastrous. Sales haven't gone up, so the marketing staff now asks the sales force to help them pinpoint possible reasons. "Is it our promotion plan? Our labeling? Our marketing plan? Our prices? Is it the lack of advertising? Is it the margin to our distributors? We are spending more money per unit on the dog food in promotion and marketing than our competitors. Why haven't we been successful?"

Finally, in the back of the room, an old salesman who has been fast asleep falls off his chair with a loud thud. Everyone in the room laughs. Hoping to embarrass the salesman, the promotion manager marches up to the microphone and says, "Mike, you are one of our oldest, most experienced salesmen. Can you answer that question?"

But Mike has seen this happen before. He had been through four previous promotion managers and six redesigns of the package. He is a survivor, so he says, "Yeah, I know the reason. The dogs won't eat the dog food."

The message is very simple. All the gimmicks and all the marketing and strategy and persuasive techniques in the world won't work unless you have a product that the customer needs.

Not Everybody Buys

Entrepreneurial persuasion requires 99 percent perspiration and 1 percent inspiration. It does not require any desperation! The entrepreneurial persuader seldom hears the word no. If you want to convince someone, my rule of thumb is that you must be willing to make at least 15 sales calls on a prospect. Only after the fifteenth call can you put the phone down and say, "OK, they don't want to buy. On to the next person." Not everyone will eat your dog food.

Ten percent of the people will never buy, no matter how often you call them. But there are 250 million people in America, and if one of them doesn't buy, that leaves another 249,999,999 prospects. So the fact that some dogs won't eat the dog food should not affect a powerful persuader with a purpose.

Selling Leadership

All good sales managers eventually face a classic dilemma, and how they respond to the challenge often determines how well they do. It's well known that the best salesperson seldom makes the best sales manager, yet companies inevitably promote their best salesperson to the position of manager. This causes a double whammy. First, the best salesperson is off the road—in that office, sales go down. Second, the sales manager is less than ideal—sales go down.

The same dilemma shows up in the sports world. A good player does not make a good manager. On the other hand, many great managers never attained great stature as players: basketball's Red Auerbach, football's Vince Lombardi, and baseball's Casey Stengel, to name a few. The great manager is seldom a great individual performer in a specific sport, whereas entrepreneurs excel as individual performers. It's rare to find them successful as managers, teachers, or trainers. Their ability to perform well with a minimal effort stands in the way of being an effective teacher or coach. A teacher or manager needs patience and self-discipline to bring the younger player along. The skills needed to be a good sales manager are often opposite to the skills needed to be a good salesperson.

Another classic sales management dilemma is: "Should I spend time with the best or worst salesperson?" There is no one answer. It depends on where you'll get the biggest return for the investment. All too often the squeaky wheel gets the oil, and the new sales manager usually errs by spending an inordinate amount of time propping up the losers. Experience argues that helping the superstars do more is a better use of time. Rainmakers work best among their peers and have trouble with subordinates who can't even create a drizzle.

Before You Lead, You Must Pace

Leading follows directly from pacing. As you establish rapport with someone, you create a link that can almost be felt. Leading comes just as naturally as pacing. You've probably experienced being with friends late at night when you're not at all tired, but you're in such deep rapport that when they yawn, you yawn too. The best salespeople do the same thing. They enter another person's world, achieve rapport, and then use that rapport to lead.

If you want a cat to sit in your lap, do you shout to the cat to come there, or do you have to coax that cat to bring him to your lap? Cat owners know the answer to this one, and they all agree you can't demand a cat do anything. People behave the same way. Ineffective persuaders can lose their prospects by being too pushy.

Pacing questions are almost always fact based. They are most effective in the form of response questions. Good persuaders are always good pacers. Pacing words have many meanings. Language is built up over time to handle all the nuances of a culture. That's why pacing questions are often specific to the culture and the language.

Language reflects a society's needs. An Eskimo has several dozen words for snow because to be an effective Eskimo, you have to be able to make fine distinctions between different kinds of snow. There is snow you can fall through, snow you can build an igloo out of, snow you can run your dogs in, snow you can eat, snow that's ready to melt.

Here are a few pacing questions:

"Is this a new location for your company?"
"How long have you been with the company?
"As I came in, I noticed a whole new department in accounting. Is that a new department, or has it just been moved here from somewhere else?"
"Is it supposed to rain today?"

Great Leaders Never Push, They Always Lead

If you have ever tried to move a piece of string across the table by pushing the string, you will observe that it balls up. But if you grab it by the other end and pull it, you can get the string to slide across the table in a straight line. That's leading, not pushing.

Here is the story of two shepherds heading two separate flocks of sheep in the Middle East. One of the shepherds moved the sheep by staying in the middle of the flock while controlling the sheep with his staff. He kept control by hitting the sheep and nudging the stragglers toward the middle. When sheep wandered, he ran out and pulled them back into the flock. At the end of the day, this type of leader is sweaty and exhausted.

The other shepherd managed to stay about a half mile ahead of his sheep, and the flock learned the direction to travel by his familiar silhouette against the skyline. No sheep ever got lost or strayed too far because the leader always stayed in clear view of the flock. This leader is seldom tired or overworked at the end of the day.

Selling Is the World's Best Profession

When I was the head of the management department faculty of Worcester Polytechnic Institute in Massachusetts, I used to ask my undergraduate students what they wanted to do when they left school. No more than two or three percent of them ever said they wanted to choose sales as a career. They always had some higher and loftier goals such as law, accounting, or another profession. When I went back and checked the alumni records of all schools, WPI included, I found that at least one quarter of all alumni are in sales. Why do young people have negative images of salespeople?

I remember when W. Clement Stone traveled with me as a CEO Club speaker in the late 1980s. The legendary founder of several insurance companies and originator of the concept of the positive mental attitude (PMA) was 85 years old during his CEO Club tour. He gave me his business card which read, "W Clement Stone, Salesman." He was most proud of that title. Too often the art of selling is downgraded because the leadership of the head salesperson is weak. You can't have a great team with a weak leader. That's why sports teams always change the managers of losing clubs.

Leadership Feedback

The single most underused element of effective sales leadership is feedback—especially positive feedback. People perform better when they have a positive self-image. Yet all too often, people get little feedback, positive or negative. This sends a message: We don't care about you. And when people feel that you don't care about them, they're not going to give their best effort. Why should they?

Tommy Lasorda, the manager of the Los Angeles Dodgers for four National League pennants and two World Series championships, told *Fortune* magazine, "Happy people give better performances. I want my players to know that I appreciate what they do for me. See, I believe in hugging my players, in patting them on the back."

People say, "God, you mean to tell me you've got a guy making a million and a half dollars a year, and you've got to motivate him!"

I say absolutely. Everybody needs to be motivated, from the president of the United States on down to the guy who works in the clubhouse.

Entrepreneurs of Today

It's the simple and the symmetrical that hold beauty. The entire universe is built on this principle: Simple ideas stand the test of time.

Even now, the physicists of the world are seeking a grand unified field theory to make their lives simple. The holy grail for these scientists is the fifth force of nature, which will combine the other four forces under one umbrella. Even Einstein sought it, but no one has found it to date. The four basic forces—gravity, electromagnetic force, weak force (atomic)*, and strong force (atomic)—have been identified for a long time, but scientists posit that four separate and isolated forces are not simple. Hence, there must be one force or one relationship that explains them all. There is an inherent logic in that appeal. It's romantic and it makes sense. Hence, the quest continues.

The same holds for persuasion. Everything important should be simple. Otherwise, it doesn't have lasting appeal.

*The weak force holds the electrons in their orbit while the strong force holds together the protons and neutrons in the nucleus.

Chapter 8

Small Business Administration Loans

Why You Should Know about the SBA

I can already hear the question in your mind: "Why is there a chapter on SBA loans in this book? SBA loans require personal guarantees, don't they?"

Well, the bad news is yes, most Small Business Administration (SBA) loans do require a personal guarantee, but the good news is that the SBA loan program is probably the best thing the federal government has ever done for entrepreneurs, and you should know about it. You probably wouldn't even pick up a book about the SBA, but now you're thinking, "Well, I guess Mancuso wouldn't waste my time with a textbook study of the SBA. He must have a few tricks to show me."

Some academics say that the SBA loan program hasn't created one major company in this country, and they're probably right, but it has financed a lot of mom-and-pop stores, a lot of restaurants, and a lot of service companies that really had no place else to go for financing. Several large companies, like Federal Express, have used SBA financing, but the critics claim this financing wasn't instrumental in the start of these growth businesses.

The SBA is a small, independent federal agency that was created by Congress in 1953 to assist, counsel, and champion small businesses. The agency has about five thousand employees in more than one hundred offices nationwide. Local offices have decision making authority in most instances.

The best way to obtain the SBA loan application package is to visit your local SBA office. If you call to order one, the office may insist that you get two loan rejections first, because the office is probably understaffed. In cities with populations of more than 200,000, you must be rejected by two lenders before you can seek a loan from the SBA.

This is a downright silly requirement, isn't it? In all my travels—and I claim to probably know more entrepreneurs than just about anyone—I've never met an entrepreneur who couldn't get turned down for a loan by a bank. I've always wondered if this requirement should be toughened up a little to something like "must be turned down by two banks within sixty days."

Going down to the local SBA office in person is a much better idea than calling. That way you can also pick up any free literature. The SBA offers a host of valuable free literature on management, support services, etc. If you ever need a quick answer about something, the **SBA hotline number is 800-8ASKSBA or 800-827-5722.**

In fiscal 1995, the SBA approved 30,000 business loans, for a total of $3.5 billion. The SBA has been making special efforts to increase the involvement of private lenders. SBA Development Company Programs, for example, offer state and local development companies special financing that enables them to extend long-term, fixed-asset financing to small businesses in their area.

The SBA Personal Guarantee

Keep in mind that you have to go on the personal guarantee for the SBA loan because the government is also on the guarantee. You can negotiate to keep your spouse off the guarantee, however, in the way I outlined in Chapter 3. The bank lends you the money and then the SBA takes a percentage of the guarantee. Usually the SBA takes 70 percent of the loan (they can take up to 90 percent), so if the loan goes bad, the SBA would step up and pay 70 percent of the loan to the bank right away. The SBA, in turn, wants your guarantee.

The interesting thing about SBA administrators, though, is that they get your personal guarantee, but they're not vicious about executing against your home. I have a very close friend who had his home up for collateral on an SBA loan for $150,000 for a solar energy company. The loan went bad, and he was able to settle with the SBA for a very reasonable payout about four years afterward. The SBA is usually pretty reasonable. They aren't quite as concerned as banks are with being paid back. Banks are dogged about getting all their money back from whatever collateral is available.

Some people think it's useful to tell the bank that you'll guarantee only the 30 percent that the bank is guaranteeing. In other words, if you borrow $100,000, the SBA will guarantee $70,000. Let's say the bank doesn't want to go along with the deal because it has to be exposed for $30,000. You can't offer to guarantee the $30,000 because it's against the law. The SBA guarantee is not $70,000 first and the bank's $30,000 second. It's pro rata, meaning out of every dollar collected, seventy cents goes to SBA and thirty cents goes to the bank.

There are some SBA direct loans that don't go through a bank, but they represent less than one percent of all SBA guaranteed loans. SBA direct loans have an administrative maximum of $150,000 and are available only to applicants unable to secure an SBA guaranteed loan. Before applying for an SBA direct loan, an applicant must first seek financing from his or her bank and, in cities with populations of more than 200,000, from at least one other lender. Direct loans usually are available only to (here is a direct allocation from Congress to encourage small business or a specific industry) businesses located in high unemployment areas, or those owned by low-income individuals, handicapped individuals, Vietnam veterans, or disabled veterans, for example. The time windows for SBA direct loans last for only about 30 days, so check the newspaper or with your local SBA office for information about these allocations to see if one comes up that might fit your business.

Most SBA loans are guaranteed loans made by private lenders (although the Money Store is the country's largest SBA lender), usually banks, and guaranteed up to 90 percent by the SBA. The maximum guarantee percentage on loans exceeding $155,000 is 85 percent. The SBA can guarantee up to $750,000 of a private sector loan. However, due to a problem in 1995, the SBA is only allowing up to $500,000.

There are three principal parties to an SBA guarantee loan: the SBA, the small business owner, and the private lender. The small business owner submits the loan application to the lender, who makes the initial review. If the lender approves it for submission to the SBA, the application is forwarded for analysis to the local SBA office. If the SBA approves the loan, the lender closes the loan and disburses the funds.

I'll tell you a secret. Banks actually like SBA loans because the bank can take that guarantee for 70 percent of the loan and turn around and sell it in the open market for cash. For example, say you borrow $100,000 from the bank, and the bank gets an SBA guarantee for $70,000. You might be paying 13 percent interest on the loan, but the bank might be able to sell the $70,000 for 9 percent because it has a government guarantee on it. The bank can make 4 percent of $70,000, but it will also get the $70,000 back to lend out again. The bank might get another SBA loan on that money and turn it around to make 4 percent of $49,000 (70 percent of $70,000 is $49,000), and so on. It's the same principle banks use to turn around home mortgages.

How to Qualify for an SBA Loan

To be eligible for SBA loan assistance, your business must operate for profit and qualify as small under SBA criteria (except for sheltered workshops under the Handicapped Assistance Loan Program). Loans cannot be made to businesses involved in the creation or distribution of ideas or opinions. This provision includes newspapers, magazines, and academic schools. Other ineligible borrowers are businesses engaged in speculation or investment in (rental) real estate.

SBA General Size Standards

Size eligibility is based on the average number of employees for the preceding twelve months or on sales volume averaged over three years.

> Manufacturing. The maximum number of employees may range from 500 to 1,500, depending on the type of product manufactured.

Wholesaling. The maximum number of employees may not exceed 500 services. Annual receipts may not exceed $3.5 to $14.5 million, depending on the industry.

Retailing. Annual receipts may not exceed $3.5 to $13.5 million, depending on the industry.

Construction. General construction annual receipts may not exceed $9.5 to $17 million, depending on the industry.

Special trade construction. Annual receipts may not exceed $7 million.

Agriculture. Annual receipts may not exceed $500,000 to $3.5 million, depending on the industry.

Here are some tips on applying for an SBA loan. First, don't let the paperwork scare you. It's really not that bad, no matter what you've heard. There are a few forms to fill out, but they are fairly straightforward. The SBA responds quickly, usually within two or three weeks.

The SBA wants to see the following:

1) A current business balance sheet listing all assets, liabilities, and net worth. New business applicants should prepare an estimated balance sheet as of the day the business starts. The amount that you and/or others have to invest in the business must be stated. The SBA requires you to show that you have an economic stake in the business.

2) Income (profit and loss) statements should be submitted for the current period and for the most recent three fiscal years, if available. New business applicants should prepare a detailed projection of earnings and expenses for the first year of operation. (A monthly cash flow is recommended.)

3) A current personal financial statement of the proprietor or each partner or stockholder owning 20 percent or more of the corporate stock. Personal guarantees are required from all the principal owners and from the chief executive officer, regardless of his or her ownership interest.

4) A list of collateral to be offered as security for the loan, along with an estimate of the present market value of each item, as well as the balance of any existing liens. SBA literature says the SBA requires that sufficient assets be pledged to adequately secure the loan to the extent that they are available. Liens on the personal assets of the principals also may be required where business assets are considered insufficient to secure the loan.

5) A statement as to the amount of the loan request and the purposes for which the loan will be used.

The SBA expects you to take this information to a bank and be turned down—then you can ask the banker to apply directly to the SBA for you. Don't think for a minute, however, that your presentation to the lender can be sloppy or inadequate. You may just be seeing her to be turned down, but she will be filling out a "lender's application" when she sends your package to the SBA. On the back of this form is a section called "lender's analysis." Your banker will give a detailed evaluation here of your debt and capital ratios, your management, your repayment of past loans, and the present state of your financials. Now you should understand why it is crucial for you to be thoroughly prepared before you see that banker.

Avoid "Little" Things That Will Slow Down Your Loan

Here are some tips on how to prepare your application for the speediest possible SBA processing:

1) Don't check the box on your application that says you paid a consultant, because if you do, your application is flagged and it might be slowed down. Your accountant is not a consultant; your lawyer is not a consultant. A consultant is not a consultant as far as SBA application is concerned. You may be getting advice from people— just don't call them consultants. The SBA uses this information to uncover illegal operations that charge

large unwarranted fees to "help" small business owners seeking SBA financing.

2) The SBA will lend you money for more than one year, unlike your friendly banker. Banks, as I'm sure you know by now, are not keen on long-term lending. At most, they like to let you borrow money on an annual basis. Banks aren't in the business of long-term lending, they are in the business of covering short-term needs. An SBA loan is one way to handle a long-term need. The typical SBA loan is for seven years. So how many years should you ask for on your application? Obviously you should ask for the maximum, seven years.

What about interest rates on SBA loans? Interest rates in the guarantee program are negotiated between the borrower and the lender, but are subject to SBA maximums. For a seven year SBA loan, the interest cannot exceed 2 percent over the New York prime, and an SBA loan with a maturity of less than seven years cannot charge interest more than 2¼ percent over the New York prime. Interest rates on direct loans are based on the cost of money to the federal government and are calculated quarterly.

3) If you ask the SBA for a seven year loan, the SBA wants to see financial projections for seven years. In some regions of the country, the SBA office will reject your loan application if you apply for a seven year loan but don't include a seven year financial projection. Imagine that! You're sitting at home, desperate for the cash, and you get a call from the SBA official, who says, "We can't process your application because you didn't forecast years six and seven, and you're asking for a seven year loan." You think to yourself, "Those guys are crazy. How am I supposed to forecast what I'm gonna do in the 21st century when I don't know what I'm gonna do tomorrow?" Then you say to the caller, "I'll tell you what you do. Take the year five projection, multiply it by 10 percent, take that projection (year six) and multiply it by 10 percent, and you'll have the seven year financial projection." Projecting for years six and seven when you submit your financials can make a difference.

4) The most money that the SBA wants you to borrow is three times what you put up. If you put up $50,000, the SBA will lend you $150,000. I have seen one case of a five-to-one debt/equity ratio, and a few cases of four-to-one and many which are two-to-one. The more common is three-to-one. This debt/equity ratio is a good balance between what's enough and what's reasonable.

5) Don't try to use the SBA to bail you out of a bad conventional loan. SBA has set a policy that it doesn't do that. So if you get a conventional loan and it goes bad, the likelihood that you can then get a SBA loan is very small. It might actually be best to start with an SBA loan because, as I said earlier, the SBA is much nicer to deal with on a bad loan than a bank. The SBA even has a fancy word for a bad loan—moratorium. A fantastically high proportion of SBA loans go through a moratorium period, there's even a form to fill out called the moratorium form. When you fill it out and submit it, you have a moratorium on your loan, i.e., you only have to make interest payments, not principal payments, for the length of the moratorium. Commercial banks have nasty lawyers who don't like moratoriums—that's why it's much nicer to deal with the SBA.

6) A lot of entrepreneurs mistakenly believe that politicians can help you get an SBA loan. A lot of politicians like to claim this is the case, but it's not true. Stay away from politicians or from big-name lawyers or accountants who say they can get your loan pushed through the SBA. The SBA has a system, and you have to wait your turn. If you try to speed up your loan approval by having a letter from a politician "friend" tacked on, the red flag will go up and your application will be slowed down.

7) If you are a manufacturer, be careful about how you classify your product. You must prove to the SBA that your product will compete successfully in the existing market, especially in its specific category. Determine the general field in which your product will best compete, then state this in your application and be prepared to substantiate your claim. The SBA uses the classification guidelines of the Standard Industrial Classification (SIC)

Manual published by the Bureau of the Budget in Washington, DC. If your product is classified incorrectly, your loan application might be rejected. For example, let's say that you manufacture an educational game, but the way you describe it in your application (by using the SIC code) leads the SBA to classify it as a toy. The price for your game is too high to be competitive in the toy market, however, so the SBA might reject your loan application. The moral of the story is *be careful,* and if in doubt about the classification of your product, talk to someone at the SBA office who can help you.

The best thing to remember about dealing with the SBA is that it was created to help the entrepreneur. The SBA has been loaning money to small business owners for more than thirty years and in all that time I doubt that it's ever taken someone's first-born child. Can your bank make the same claim? Both have foreclosed on homes, but the SBA takes longer to do it and is a bit more gentle. Of course, it hurts just the same. I put all this information on the SBA into this book because I really think it's a worthwhile source of financing. At the very least, visit your local SBA office and pick up some of that free literature. You might learn something, and six weeks from now you might have a loan!

Every community has some bank that is involved with the SBA's preferred lender program (PLP). In Chicago, for example, there are banks that have been identified as SBA banks. They have already advanced in Washington, DC, at SBA headquarters, a certain amount of money to be held in escrow should they make any bad SBA debts. This allows these banks to approve SBA loans right from the bank, because they're now qualified as members of PLP. If you're going to apply for an SBA loan, it obviously makes sense to apply at a PLP bank because the PLP bank can approve your loan simultaneously as the bank and as a representative of the SBA. It's quicker than going through the bank and then through the SBA. To find out what bank in your community is a PLP bank, call the SBA hotline number (800-827-5722), ask your banker, or ask your accountant or lawyer.

Don't Believe All Those Myths about SBA Loans

Probably the most common myth is that SBA loans take forever to be approved. Don't be fooled by the entrepreneur's traditional mistrust of bureaucracy into thinking this is true. An entrepreneur I know, Joe Maroni, owner of the Northworks restaurant in Worcester, Massachusetts, got an SBA loan processed in about five weeks. He submitted his business plan (see his full business plan in my book *How to Prepare and Present a Business Plan*), filled out the forms, and got a four-to-one debt ratio. In other words, he put up $50,000 and got $200,000 within five weeks. The average time from your presentation of a well-prepared loan package to your banker to the moment you receive your SBA check ranges from three to six months in the real world.

People tell me an SBA loan can't be done quickly, but it can if you know how to prepare your application so that it doesn't get stuck in any files on its way through the SBA office. The chief factor in the expedition of your loan request is the completeness of your loan application. If your application is inadequate, the SBA will keep rejecting it until it meets the agency's minimum standards.

The SBA examines not only all aspects of the business venture but also the applicant's personal qualifications. Three qualifications are considered essential:

1) You must have an economic stake in the venture. A stake is not collateral, nor is it time invested in the business. You must show that you have made an economic contribution to the business. You are expected to have contributed 20 percent to 30 percent when purchasing an existing business and 30 percent to 50 percent when you are starting a business from scratch.
2) You must be able to present a lease agreement. Your lease agreement should be for at least the period of the loan you are requesting.
3) You must show some collateral.

The SBA looks at several other factors when it runs its evaluation analysis, but these three are the most important personal qualifications.

The SBA divides its loans into three categories: loans for the start-up of a business, loans for the purchase of a business, and loans for the expansion of an existing business. Here is a list of the documents required from applicants in all loan categories:

1) Two loan rejections from two acceptable lenders
2) SBA loan application
3) Statement of personal history
4) Personal financial statement
5) Summary of collateral
6) Operating plan forecast
7) Cash flow projections
8) Resume and work experience
9) Copy of lease agreement
10) Business plan

Another SBA myth that dies hard is that "only minorities get SBA loans." The fact is, the amount of SBA guaranteed loans to minorities is approximately proportionate to minorities' representation in the U.S. population.

The myth that SBA loans require too much paperwork and struggles with red tape has, I hope, been debunked by what you've read so far. The documentation requirements for SBA loans don't differ much from those for a regular commercial bank loan. The SBA makes it easier, in fact, by providing a complete loan application that makes your obligations quite clear (in other words, the SBA doesn't delight in playing go-fetch the way your banker does). You may think that both banks and the SBA are too demanding, but take my word for it, you ain't seen nothing until you deal with a venture capital firm. Requirements will be far more demanding.

Index

A

accountants, 7, 176
advertising agencies, 5–7

B

bank loan
  document preparation, 98, negotiating, 88–90, renewing, 75–76,
  repayment, 75, request, 74–75,
  troublesome provisions, 88
bankers, 6–7
  characteristics, 73–74, 181–85
  questions for, 74
bankrupt companies, 103
banks, communicating with, 78–79
board of directors, 8–10, 49
brokers, 138
business plan
  definition, 21–22, overcoming
  negatives, 42–46, 53, preparation, 21–23, 27–29, presenting,
  52–53, 59–62, purpose, 20–21
  questionnaire, 29–32, 39–41
  reading of, 24–27
business purchase
  assets, 115–16, business history,
  110, closing, 107, financial
  checklist, 107–9,
  investigating, 107, real estate,
  115–16

C

capital
  commitment, 53–54, 62–63, for
  entrepreneurs, 51–54, prospecting, 52, 55–58, when to raise,
  49–51, 82–83
capital source, qualifying, 51–54,
  58–60
collateral, 97, 206
company background, 150
company salespeople, 12
competition, 105, 110–13
controller, 12–14
corporate logo, 5–6
corporate strategy, 65–66
credit, requirements, 96–97

E

earnings claims, 165–66
emotion, 141–42

F

employees, 118–19
entrepreneur first mate, 14–16,
  motivation, 16–17, synergy,
  17–18, vs. manager, 180
entrepreneurial team, 2–3, 30
entrepreneur's quiz, 125–31

fads, 153
feedback, 199–200
feel, felt, found technique, 61–62,
  190
financial acumen, 136
financials, preparation, 32–36
franchise
  advertising, 154, closing, 177
  competition, 157–58, financing
  sources, 175–76,
  how to finance, 174–76,
  initial fees, 171–72,
  location, 156, management, 156
  new, 171–72, offering circular,
  162, 166–67, risk, 139–41,
  167–69, risk vs. return, 139, royalties, 171–74, selecting,
  137, service-type, 171–72,
  support, 154, system, 155–56,
  territory, 158, waiting
  period, 166, 176–77, working
  capital, 159, franchise test,
  125–31, franchise brochure,
  148–51, reading of, 149–51,
  franchise candidates, 145–48,
  151–52, franchise source guides,
  147–48, franchise trade shows,
  147, franchisee, aptitude,
  123–25, hours, 132, people
  skills, 132–33, sales ability, 133,
  traits, 131–36
franchises to avoid, 153–54
franchising, investment, 166–74
franchisor, visiting, 160–62

G

godfather, 4

H

homestead, protecting, 95–96
Homestead Act, 8, 95–96
horizontal search, 144–45

About the Author

Joseph R. Mancuso is recognized as America's bestselling small business book author and leading entrepreneurial expert. As founder and President of the Center for Entrepreneurial Management and the Chief Executive Officers Club, he has his finger on the pulse of the American small business.

With over 3,000 members, the Center for Entrepreneurial Management is the world's largest nonprofit association of entrepreneurs. The Chief Executive Officers Club, with membership consisting of CEOs of companies above $2,000,000 in annual sales, has chapters in 12 major cities. Mancuso founded these organizations to act as a forum to grow the ideas and overcome the obstacles of small businesses. The wealth of information and experience Mancuso has developed and imparted through these organizations is unsurpassed.

Mancuso has founded seven businesses and is a member of the board of directors for forty diverse U.S. companies. In addition, he is an investor and director of several successful private and public companies. He is, however, probably best known as an author. He has written 22 management and small business books, many of which are also available on audio or video cassettes. He is the author of *Mancuso's Small Business Resource Guide*, also published by Sourcebooks.

Mancuso holds an Electrical Engineering degree from W.P.I., an MBA from the Harvard Business School, and a Doctorate in Educational Administration from Boston University. He lives in Manhattan with his wife and business partner Karla, and their two children Max and May.